D0760410
VED
NOV 2019
By

Advance Praise for

Life at 8 mph

"Peter Anderson has written an honest, unsentimental, sometimes terribly funny and deeply poignant account of lasting friendship..."

—Dr. Rosalie de Rosset, author of *Unseduced and Unshaken: The Place of Dignity in a Young Woman's Choices* and Professor of Communications and Literature, Moody Bible Institute

"Far more than an engrossing read, it offers real-life tools for finding your own happily-ever-after—accessible tools, made for imperfect people. This book is for everyone whose heart beats. Anyone. Anywhere. Of any race, gender, or economic situation. I feel blessed for having read it."

—Tara Taylor Quinn, *USA Today* bestselling author

"Laced with rich wit and wisdom ... a profoundly different philosophy that might change the way everyone views their struggles."

—Lyla Swafford, author of *It Takes More Than Legs to Stand*

Life at 8 mph

How a Man with Cerebral Palsy Taught Me the Secret to Happiness

Peter Bowling Anderson

Cover and book design by Mark Sullivan
Cover illustration by Rebecca Hipp

ISBN 978-0-9997422-7-3 (paperback)
ISBN 978-0-9997422-8-0 (e-book)

Library of Congress Cataloging-in-Publication Data
Names: Anderson, Peter Bowling, author.
Title: Life at 8 mph : how a man with cerebral palsy taught me the secret to happiness / by Peter Bowling Anderson.
Other titles: Life at eight miles per hour
Description: Georgetown, Ohio : KiCam Projects, [2018].
Identifiers: LCCN 2019000135 (print) | LCCN 2019007901 (ebook) | ISBN 9780999742280 (ebook) | ISBN 9780999742273 | ISBN 9780999742273(paperback)
Subjects: LCSH: Anderson, Peter Bowling. | Male caregivers–United States–Biography. | Herrin, Richard (Reverend) | Cerebral palsied–United
States–Biography. | Clergy with disabilities–United States–Biography. | Christian men–United States–Biography. | Male friendship.
Classification: LCC RC388 (ebook) | LCC RC388 .A53 2018 (print) | DDC 616.8/360092 [B] –dc23
LC record available at https://lccn.loc.gov/2019000135

Printed in the United States of America

Published by KiCam Projects
Georgetown, Ohio

www.KiCamProjects.com

For Mom,
who stood up more than she sat down at dinner.

CONTENTS

“Our destiny is frequently met in the
very paths we take to avoid it.”

Jean de la Fontaine

CHAPTER ONE

Mr. Persistent

The only thing I knew for certain was I didn't want to work for him. It took me all of two minutes to reach that conclusion.

I'd come to Richard Herrin's small, two-bedroom duplex on Wheaton Street, just around the corner from a nearly empty Chinese restaurant and a packed Whataburger, because I needed a job, any job, and I was desperate. I'd been in Fort Worth for over a month, with nothing panning out. I needed a full-time job to cover my bills, yet something kept nixing each prospect, leaving me increasingly dispirited. One day in the lounge of my roommate's graduate school, I saw a notice for a tutoring job. The position was only for ten hours a week, so I grabbed a tab and forgot about it until that night when emptying my pockets. After another unsuccessful day of job hunting, I thought it might be time to adopt a different strategy. I read the tab again: REV. RICHARD HERRIN SEEKS TUTOR, 10 HOURS WEEKLY, GRADUATE STUDIES. I knew of another part-time job I thought I could get, and I was just starting to play in a band in Dallas. Perhaps between the three jobs, I'd be okay.

I called the number on the tab, and a severely slurred voice answered. I said, "Hello," hoping the connection would clear.

Yet I heard the same, garbled, indecipherable response. This wasn't a poor connection. Somewhere inside me, the first alarm rang out. There would be many more. I tried saying hello again but was met with a string of slurred speech that overwhelmed me. I considered hanging up, before I heard the first word I understood: "Richard."

I introduced myself and told him I'd seen his job notice, and I asked if he'd like to meet. What I really wanted to ask was what was wrong with him, because I couldn't follow a word he was saying.

But then I heard it—the second word I understood—and this one made a much more profound impact on me than his name.

"Palsy."

I almost dropped the phone, partly because I feared it might be contagious through the connection (I was a bit of a germaphobe, to say the least), and partly because I knew what that word meant. I certainly wasn't an expert on cerebral palsy, yet I'd seen people on TV with it and read a few stories and I instantly understood I'd already bitten off far more than I could chew. This tutoring position was going to be much more than I could handle.

I stammered, "Listen…uh…I'm sorry for bothering you. I need to go…now…"

Yet with the persistence to which I'd soon become accustomed, Richard cut me off and said the first full sentence I grasped: "Can you come tomorrow?"

I shook my head as if he could see me or to remind myself of the correct answer, though what tumbled out of my mouth was something entirely different. Undoubtedly born from my exhaustive, fruitless job search, I answered, "Yeah, I can do that."

Richard had to repeat his address eight times before I copied it all down correctly, but the next day at 10 a.m. I was at his home near East Gourmet Buffet, the sleepy Chinese restaurant, totally unprepared for what I was about to experience.

I knocked on his peeling, beige door, yet no one answered. I knocked again but heard nothing. A wave of euphoria swept over me. I wanted to scream, *Yes! I've been released!!!* I'd done the right thing and faced my fears and come despite not wanting anything to do with this terrifying situation, and now I could return to the want ads with a clear conscience. I turned to leave, when it happened.

The door opened.

By itself.

It was like something out of a horror movie. The door even creaked. There was a rope tied to the inside handle pulling the door open. I halfway expected a mummy to stagger out wielding a hatchet. *I'm not going in there,* I swore to myself. *We can just meet outside. I'm fine right here.*

This was the first of roughly two thousand times I heard Richard's motorized wheelchair approach. I didn't know what to expect, though I'd seen people with cerebral palsy before. For some reason, I couldn't get the image out of my head of a masked Hannibal Lecter being wheeled out on a dolly. If he cracked, "Love your suit," I was sprinting to my car.

Then Richard appeared in the doorway, his mouth hanging open, his torso slumped to his left in his dull black wheelchair, his fingers curled as if he was trying to ball them into fists but they'd frozen in transit. His short brown hair was parted to the left, his face clean-shaven and pale, and he wore navy blue dress pants and a long-sleeve, white dress shirt stretched over a small potbelly. My eyes returned to his gnarled fingers. His right hand rested on his wheelchair's joystick that directed the chair's movement and, as I later discovered, allowed him to recline as far back as a dentist's chair, while his left hand waved at me. Instinctively, I took a slight step backward in his driveway. But Richard wasn't going to let me get away that easily. He lurched out of his duplex in his motorized wheelchair straight for me. I realized that even if I tried to race to my car, he could chase me down. There was no way out. He'd trapped me as soon as I'd exited my car. This was the moment I was certain I didn't want to work for him.

Richard had an orange light on his chair, like on top of a tow truck, which sat on a pole behind his left shoulder. It wasn't on, but I could picture it flashing and rotating as he sped down the street. It must've been quite a sight. I wondered if he had a siren. Richard was forty-six when we met that hazy, sweltering June morning in his driveway, though when he smiled, he looked closer to forty. I had to admit, he had quite a smile, an engaging, welcoming smile, the kind that made me forget all about his cerebral palsy, if only for a moment.

I introduced myself and reminded him of our conversation on the phone, though he just laughed and replied, "You're not selling Bibles?"

I wasn't sure I'd heard him correctly. His speech was very slurred, yet it sounded like he'd made a joke. I took the safe route and repeated my introduction, almost verbatim.

He began laughing so hard, drool spilled out of the left corner of his mouth. Then he flicked the joystick with his right index finger to make his wheelchair spin around in a circle, as he exclaimed, "I've got cerebral palsy; I'm not crazy!"

I couldn't help but chuckle. For a moment, we both just

stared at each other, smiling.

I decided it was safe to follow him inside his home, where his service dog, Troy Aikman (his trainers had named him after the Cowboys' old quarterback), greeted me. However, Richard snapped, "Aaaagh," for Troy to stop licking my hands. Richard then said, "Door," and Troy hustled over to the wall and poked a button with his nose to automatically close his front door. I was impressed. Richard zipped down a ramp from his dining room to his living room, waved me over to the couch, and then proceeded to spend the next ten minutes trying to explain why I couldn't pet Troy or look at him or speak to him or acknowledge his presence in any way. Troy was a two-year-old Golden Retriever that had received extensive special training to service Richard's unique needs. He could pick up items Richard dropped, bring his own leash and service vest to Richard if they were headed out, open and close doors, and provide companionship and affection that Richard sorely needed. All of this training cost $20,000, for which Richard had to do considerable fundraising, and it could be ruined, or at least severely compromised, if Troy started bonding with someone other than Richard.

So I couldn't pet Troy, ever, even though he was gorgeous, incredibly friendly, and I'd grown up in a house full of dogs and dog lovers. My family used to let our furry friends sleep on our beds, when they weren't finishing our meals or watching TV next to us on the couch. Now I was potentially going to sit next to a sweet pooch each day that I couldn't give belly rubs or scratch behind his ears or sneak treats. Talk about torture. This was another strike against taking the job.

Richard endeavored to explain how he needed my help, repeating himself over and over, but I struggled mightily to comprehend. I could tell he was growing frustrated, and I couldn't blame him. How hard would it have been to spend all day every single day trying to get people to understand? I would've been exhausted and seriously contemplated becoming a shut-in.

Finally, after what felt like half an hour, I was able to deduce that he needed a tutor to help him with an online master's degree in religion/counseling that he was working on through a Christian college, and that he'd just started the program.

He stared at me with his head cocked to his left waiting for my answer. I smiled. Troy began wagging his tail, so I immediately looked at the plant in the corner so Richard didn't think I was smiling at his dog. Suddenly, the living room felt very warm. I didn't know what to tell Richard, or at least *how* to say it. I didn't want the job. I thought our communication would be far too difficult and time-consuming to meet assignment deadlines, but I didn't want to hurt his feelings or crush his spirit. It was obvious he was very enthusiastic about his new degree program. If I didn't help him, would anyone else? Would he just give up? Was that the right reason to take the job? Was it safe to stop watching the plant yet?

I decided to buy myself time, so I answered, "Can I pray about it?" Since he was a reverend, this seemed like a safe, positive response.

However, Richard merely raised his eyebrows and asked, "You wanna pray right now?" Then he added a smile to convince me. He should've been a used-car salesman.

"Uh…actually…uh…I have another appointment to get to," I semi-lied. I had to buy toothpaste and shaving cream on the way home. That was sort of like an appointment.

He turned up the wattage on his smile to full power and said, "You sure?"

I stood to gain momentum for the door while nodding very quickly like a bobblehead doll. "Yeah, I need to go. But thank you so much for seeing me. I'll call you by the end of the week with my answer. Is that okay?"

Not for Mr. Persistent. Not even close. He said, "Can you call tomorrow? I'm behind in school." He crept closer in his wheelchair with the most desperate look on his face, like his life literally clung to my decision. I was sweating through my Polo shirt. I had no idea what to say, so, naturally, I agreed. When inconvenient, the truth rarely volunteered itself; it had to be dragged out kicking and screaming, claws and all.

On the way home, I dug around in my pocket and pulled out the little tab I'd yanked off Richard's Help Wanted ad in the lounge. I remembered seeing another name at the bottom of the slip of paper. "With additional questions, please contact Mike Shreve." As soon as I got home, I called Mike to learn a little more about Richard and his situation. Even though I didn't want the job, my conscience was holding me hostage. I just couldn't say no without finding out Richard's options.

Thankfully, Mike was very informative and helpful. At the time, he worked at the graduate school and had posted Richard's want ad in the lounge. He'd known Richard for a few years. He told me Richard was divorced with three kids and that his youngest son, Michael, lived with Richard, though I hadn't seen him in the home. The other kids lived with relatives in the country. He said Richard employed three attendants, but the one who'd worked with him for the last three years was quitting because of a new job. I let that sink in for a second...three years. I didn't see how that was possible. That attendant must've had a true servant's heart and an inexhaustible supply of patience I didn't possess.

Richard had had it pretty rough growing up. He was born in Texas, but his parents got divorced when he was a baby and his mother moved him to Oklahoma. He lived with his mother until he was seven, but then she shipped him back to Texas to live with his dad because she was tired of dealing with the struggles and inconveniences of someone with CP confined to a wheelchair.

His dad placed him in a children's hospital that concentrated on teaching and rehabbing physically challenged children. When Richard aged out of that facility at fourteen, his dad put him in another school for cerebral palsied children until Richard turned sixteen. Both of these facilities were about four hours from Richard's father's house, and his dad allowed him to return home only at Christmas and for two weeks during the summers. At sixteen, Richard aged out of the second facility and had to start high school at McKinney High near his dad's house. This was the first time Richard lived full-time with his father, and as with Richard's mother, this ultimately wore out his dad. Richard attended high school until he was twenty-one and aged out. He didn't receive a diploma, and by then, his dad was burned out and placed Richard in an institution for the mentally challenged, even though Richard didn't suffer from this disability.

When Richard finally got out of the institution, he bounced in and out of nursing homes for a few years but was able to get into Section 8 housing, receive meager government assistance and food stamps, and start living on his own with the help of attendants through the CLASS (Community Living Assistance and Support Services) program. During these years, Richard earned his GED and became an ordained minister. Eventually, he attended Texas Wesleyan College, where he earned a degree in liberal arts. He'd wanted to major in counseling, but the head of the department had made it so complicated for Richard that he and his advisor decided to switch to a liberal arts degree.

Richard also met a woman with cerebral palsy at a park where Reach, a group that helped physically challenged people live on their own, was hosting a picnic. The two were married for fourteen years and had three children, but then she cheated on Richard and they divorced. After that, his two oldest kids, Nathan and Charity, went to live with relatives in the country, while Michael lived with Richard. They moved a few times and had been living at the duplex on Wheaton Street where I met Richard for about a year. Michael was now ten.

I shook my head and exhaled, trying to process it all. It was a lot to absorb. Richard was certainly more resilient than I.

Since Richard was an ordained minister, I asked Mike if he pastored a church. Mike said, "No, but if you need to get married in a pinch, he can help you out."

"Ah, no, no, I'm good in that department," I quickly answered. I wasn't ready to get married, and besides, I didn't even have a girlfriend. I couldn't find a job, I was living in the spare bedroom of my friend's parents' house, and we shared a car with a bad muffler and 203,000 miles on it. Marriage was currently near the bottom of my to-do list.

Before I hung up, I asked Mike one last question, since he'd been friends with Richard for several years. "How long did it take you to understand Richard's speech without any difficulty?"

Mike said, "Without *any* difficulty? I'm still working on that. But you'll get the hang of it. Don't worry—you'll catch on pretty quickly. You two will hit it off."

He made it sound like I already worked for Richard.

After we said goodbye, I wrote out a list of pros and cons for the job. I thought of quite a few cons but only one pro. I studied my list and then put it in a drawer because it was depressing. The only pro seemed to outweigh all the cons, no matter their merit.

Since I was on the clock and had to make a decision by tomorrow, I decided to keep my word and actually do what I'd told Richard I needed time to do: I prayed to God for guidance and wisdom to make the right choice, because I needed it big time. My biggest fear was that if I agreed to work for Richard, I'd bail out after a few weeks and let him down, and though I didn't know him, it was clear he'd already been let down too many times. If I was going to disappoint him, sooner was far kinder than later.

The next morning, I called Richard and told him yes.

It surprised even me. The one pro, money, had tilted the balance, as did perhaps my dread of a guilty conscience. Nothing motivated quite as powerfully as guilt or fear. This time, guilt won.

Of course, I never could've guessed at the time, but that was the beginning of five years of working with Richard. And as much as Richard needed my help, I needed his more.

CHAPTER TWO

The Outsider

My first day working with Richard was enlightening, to say the least. I wasn't sure how to dress, so since he'd worn a business shirt and slacks for our interview, I dusted off the only suit I owned and wore it to his home. It was 102 degrees outside and the air conditioner in my car had conceded defeat. By the time I walked into Richard's duplex, I was soaked with sweat. Not a good start to the day. To drive home the point that I'd overdressed, Richard looked over my attire and teased, "You getting married?" He started laughing so hard, he began coughing violently. I thought he was about to die under my care on my first day. Was I supposed to call 911? Do the Heimlich maneuver? Get out of the way so Troy Aikman could hopefully save the day? I jumped up and held his giant water bottle, a sixty-four-ounce Conoco cup with a sturdy handle and a long, bendable plastic hose of a straw, under his mouth so he could drink some water to slow the dying process. He took a sip, but brown liquid flowed through the straw. I later learned that Richard's favorite drink was sweet tea, and he rarely drank "boring" water, as he put it.

Once his hacking subsided and I'd gotten my heart rate down, he smiled and garbled something about how he coughed a lot when laughing and that I'd get used to it. I was just glad he didn't die.

I filled out the long application, which he said was a formality but required by his payroll company for a background check, and then he showed me around his home. The kitchen was small but clean, as was the hall bathroom. His night attendant took care of the cleaning and got him ready for bed, while his morning attendant showered him and prepared him for the day. Suddenly, my shift looked like the best slot in the rotation. As a card-carrying germaphobe, helping someone use the bathroom was just above licking beef stew off the street.

Michael's room was the messiest in the duplex, but that was a kid's duty. As Richard showed me around, I wondered how his morning attendant showered him and how both caregivers got him in and out of bed. Were they power lifters weighing three hundred pounds each? Was I ever expected to hoist Richard out of his chair or into my car? Was back surgery covered in the contract I'd just signed?

And wait a minute—was I going to have to help him use the bathroom?!!!

Dear God, I'm going to pass out, I thought, feeling lightheaded.

As if he were reading my mind, Richard told me to look up at the ceiling in his bedroom. In addition to a water stain or two, I saw a track running along the ceiling from his bed to his bathroom. He positioned his chair underneath the end of the track and hit a button on a remote that lowered a metal handle that looked like a large hanger with hooks. It took a while for me to understand what was supposed to happen next, but two of the three wide straps hanging from the hooks were placed underneath his hamstrings and their ends pulled up to fasten to the outside hooks, while the widest strap slipped around his back and under his arms and then fastened to the inner hooks. And then a button on the remote lifted him up out of his chair like a stork carrying a new baby. That was how his attendants transported him in and out of his wheelchair, bed, and bathroom. The track and straps did all the heavy lifting for them, which was a relief.

I joked, "I'm glad, because my back was already hurting thinking about trying to lift you out of that chair."

Richard grew very serious and concerned, and said, "You can't. You'd get hurt lifting my fat butt...and so would I."

I nodded, and replied, "Don't worry. I only lift people on the weekends."

He grinned, and said, "Okay. Okay."

He led me back to his living room to his work station. I sat down at his computer, and he showed me where his class assignments were online. I wasn't used to operating a Mac, and the flat mouse on the keypad felt awkward and hypersensitive. I was afraid to touch it. It was like I was typing on an ice skating rink. However, Richard's cerebral palsy had ravaged his fingers so much that he couldn't operate an old-fashioned mouse. His right index finger was the only digit he used for his wheelchair's joystick and for his computer. When he tried to type something, he implemented a slow-motion version of hunt and peck.

I read through his first class's syllabus, when I noticed something extremely disturbing: The class was over in three days, and he'd yet to turn in anything! I just stared at the screen for a few moments hoping a flood of assignments would instantly post. Not one test? No papers? Nothing? I slowly turned to Richard while forcing a smile. He smiled back. I peeked at the screen. Nope, still no assignments.

Not only had Richard almost died on my first day, but he was going to flunk school, too. I was beginning to understand why the other guy left.

But what about the other fella? Surely they'd done *some* work together. "Richard, did you and your other attendants work on any of these assignments? Do you have any rough drafts you're writing?" Pretty please.

His chair sprang to life as he rolled to the computer, and I gladly scooted away from his academic disaster zone. After touching a few buttons, a document appeared. It was a paper, or more accurately, a sermon, rife with grammatical errors and, at times, incoherent. "This is my paper for class," he explained.

I nodded repeatedly while scrolling through, hoping to reassure him while trying to figure out how I could quit without devastating him. This was a lost cause. The paper needed to be completely rewritten, and it was only one assignment. I asked Richard, "What about the other things due?"

Then he pushed a few more buttons and showed me the percentages assigned to each project. The paper was a huge chunk of his grade. Though he hadn't turned in anything else, if he managed to get an "A" on his paper, he would barely pass the course. "See," he said.

I did see. It was the bottom of the ninth, two outs, and we needed a grand slam on the final pitch or he was getting placed on academic probation or possibly dropped from the program. That would mean my tutoring hours probably would disappear.

I turned back to Richard, who still had his movie star smile plastered across his face. Yet I couldn't help but notice a trace of desperation in his eyes. He knew I was his last chance at passing. Still, I had to be honest with him, and I said, "I'm sorry, Richard, but I…I just don't think this is doable. Not in the amount of time left."

I literally started patting my pockets as subtly as possible to make sure I had my wallet and keys. I was done. It hadn't worked out, and that was that. He didn't need a tutor, he needed a do-over in life because his was an endless series of unfair and unlucky breaks, betrayals, and heartaches, and this was the latest. But just as I was about to push away from the computer to stand to deliver the crushing news to Richard, he simply asked, "Can't we try?"

He might as well have handcuffed me to my chair and barred his front door, because after that, I couldn't go anywhere. There was no leaving now. How in the world could I have said no to that? He'd trapped me again just by being himself. It was almost amusing. I wondered if this would be a daily occurrence.

Richard had received permission from his professor to write the paper in sermon format (after all, it was a Christian school), so at least that was acceptable. Now I just needed to start from scratch with Richard and edit as we went. Since we had only three days, I set a goal for us to finish a third of the paper by the end of the day, which meant we were in for a lot of work.

I didn't realize the battle would be waged on two fronts.

Richard hated being cooped up, and I couldn't blame him. If I'd spent my whole life crammed in a wheelchair unable to walk, I would've craved mobility, too. Plus, Richard was a minister, a people person, so he wanted to be out and about interacting with his community. However, while I sympathized with him and completely understood his yearnings, we needed to stay put and work relentlessly on the paper if we were going to have any chance of completing it in time and earning an "A." But after an hour and a half of painstakingly translating and editing Richard's thoughts into his sermon, he got a phone call. And then another call about ten minutes later from the repairman who worked on his wheelchair. They talked for a good twenty-five minutes. Then Richard needed me to send an email to his mentor at the seminary, which took quite a while. Then another call. And another two emails.

Then it was lunchtime. He asked if I was hungry because it was time to eat. There went half the day.

As we emerged from Richard's dimly lit duplex into the blinding midday sun, my mood rapidly deteriorated. I was already sweating in my stupid suit, I didn't know where we were walking, and we'd barely finished the first page of his paper. It was supposed to be fifteen to twenty pages long. We didn't have a prayer.

I followed behind Richard and Troy as they led the way down the street. Troy wore his snazzy red service dog vest and seemed just as excited as Richard to be uncaged. I felt like a third wheel on their date. I still didn't know where we were headed, but I guessed/hoped East Gourmet Buffet on the corner. The blast furnace that is Fort Worth in the summer was too unforgiving for a longer walk. Richard didn't own a wheelchair-accessible van—or any vehicle, for that matter—so we'd be walking or riding the bus everywhere.

Thankfully, Richard lived near a strip mall just across the railroad tracks that had everything from a pet store to a grocery store to another Chinese restaurant. I never knew Asian cuisine was so popular in Fort Worth. Ten years earlier, I'd lived here while attending seminary, but after graduating with a master's in communications, I moved with two schoolmates to Atlanta to pursue a band we'd started. I hadn't returned since. It looked the same but different, as any place did after enough time and space. My perspective had changed since school, perhaps less optimistic or more realistic regarding the world's offerings, depending on my cynicism that day. One thing I'd learned for certain was that a dream rarely materialized to code; it came with leaky pipes and shoddy wiring and usually didn't offer a second walk-through.

I gladly held open the door to East Gourmet Buffet for Richard and Troy as we escaped the heat. I'd never walked into a restaurant with a dog and I was a little nervous we'd be kicked out. But the hostess smiled at Richard and quickly ushered us to a table. I could tell Richard had been here before, and when the waitress immediately took his Conoco water bottle to refill his sweet tea, I knew he was a regular.

I'd brought along my sack with a little bag of chips and two cookies, my daily lunch on a shoestring budget, and opened it on our table. I didn't have enough money to eat out, and I certainly wasn't assuming Richard was treating. He lived on his own tight budget with nothing extra to spare.

Yet that was exactly what he did.

He saw my sad little meal and shook his head and smiled. "You gonna feed the birds?"

I laughed out loud at that one. He did have a good sense of humor. I said, "No, this is my lunch. You go ahead. I'm good."

In about a nanosecond, he was beside me, tugging my arm. "Come on, you're eating food today," he ordered.

I stood up and followed him and Troy over to the buffet spread. There were heated trays of egg rolls, fried shrimp, beef and vegetable mixes, soups, egg foo young, and on and on. I didn't know where to begin. Then I saw the dessert table with cookies, cakes, and three kinds of pudding. I almost started drooling. I looked down at Richard, but he just smiled, waiting. Then I remembered I was there to help *him.* "Oh, okay, what would you like?"

There were only five other guests in the restaurant, and none of them seemed too interested in us. Perhaps they were also regulars and had seen Richard and his dog many times. The staff acted like nothing was out of the ordinary. It dawned on me that I'd entered Richard's world and not the other way around. I was the outsider, the unfamiliar face, and he'd survived for years on his own before I showed up. I was going to have to adapt, not him. I had plenty of insecurities and inhibitions that were all going to be put to a serious test working for him. And it scared me to death. I wanted to drop the plate and run straight out the door, but Troy would've eaten the food and ruined his strict service dog diet. Besides, Richard wanted some more gravy on his egg foo young.

That afternoon I met Michael, Richard's youngest son. He was ten and attended an elementary school four blocks away. Richard told me he needed to break from working on the paper to go pick him up, and he asked if I wanted to follow in my car. At first, I didn't understand. "Do you want me to drive him home?" I asked.

"You gonna give me a ride, too?" he said with a snort and a cough.

"Huh?" I asked, thoroughly confused.

"Follow me," he said with a wave and another snort as he charged up the ramp to his front door.

I drove behind Richard with my flashers on the whole way to the school. I was going eight miles an hour (Richard's max speed) and was terrified I'd rear-end him. He was going much faster than when we'd walked to the restaurant, so there was no way I could've kept up with him without driving. He didn't want to make Michael wait, which I thought was considerate.

I pulled into the long line of cars in front of the school with parents waiting for kids, while Richard snaked his way through the crowd to meet Michael. I still wasn't sure how we were transporting Michael home, or when that might be. I was at the back of a very long line. Richard passing his class seemed more hopeless by the minute.

Then I saw them, but it wasn't what I'd expected.

Richard barreled out of the school weaving his way through the throng of parents and kids like a downhill skier on the giant slalom, as Michael reclined on his dad's lap like he was in a La-Z-Boy watching cartoons. All Michael needed was popcorn. As they approached my car, Michael looked completely relaxed, as if this were a normal, everyday occurrence with no cause for alarm. Of course, I later learned it was. Perhaps he was trying to calm me down, because all I kept thinking was, *If he tumbles out of that chair and Richard runs him over, I was never here.* I glanced around for my quickest escape route.

Michael looked like a mini-Richard, just without CP. Same nose, eyes, hair. He was smiling when they pulled up next to my car. "This is Michael," Richard boasted with a huge smile.

I introduced myself, but before our chitchatting got carried away, Richard instructed, "Follow me," and took off. I trailed with my hazards on again, though I did notice he was motoring a tad slower with precious cargo in tow.

When we returned to Richard's duplex, I asked Michael how long his dad had been shuttling him to school and how it began. I asked him if they ever went off-roading. I asked what he and his dad talked about as they drove. Yet I unexpectedly stumbled on a landmine. Richard had been steadily boiling and finally growled, "Ask me!" I looked at Richard, and his Hollywood smile was long gone. Lasers shot out of his eyes straight through me, while his right index finger rested on his chair's joystick like he was a bull set to charge.

"Sorry?" was all I could muster.

"You ask me! You wanna know something 'bout me, ask me," Richard snapped, eyeing me for the slightest trace of defiance.

Fearing for my life, I nodded and immediately answered, "Yes, sir."

I soon learned this was a cardinal sin, one of the most aggravating and intolerable aspects of Richard's life with cerebral palsy. Richard loved talking to people, but his speech impairment made it difficult for them to understand him. Most gave up after a short time and simply directed their questions to the attendant, friend, or family member accompanying Richard. It made him feel invisible and insignificant, like he wasn't worth the time and effort required to comprehend his words.

Unfortunately, I was a slow study and committed this same offense a few more painful times before finally learning my lesson.

Richard told me he'd been carrying Michael to and from school since they'd moved to their current home. He said Michael enjoyed it, and it was obvious Richard did. Clearly, it gave him a sense of fulfillment to be able to offer his son something special. Richard even added, already in better spirits, "I might talk funny, but I'm the fastest dad in town."

It turned out I wasn't the only one impressed with Richard hauling Michael around. A neighbor and cameraman for a local news station saw the two of them scooting up the street to school a few mornings before I started. Intrigued, he popped by Richard's duplex that evening to learn more. He was so taken with Richard and Michael, he pitched their story to a reporter at his station. Richard informed me the reporter was coming tomorrow to interview Michael and him.

"Tomorrow?" I asked, stunned that I was talking to a future star, while mourning the loss of more paper time.

Tomorrow, indeed. The reporter and cameraman arrived the following afternoon at three so they could film Richard, Michael, and Troy parading down Wheaton Street from school. A few curious neighbors poked their heads out their doors to see the spectacle. Michael waved to them, as Richard's orange light glowed and spun. I wished I had confetti to toss.

We all then convened in Richard's living room for the interview, which was punctuated by Richard hollering at Troy to stop licking the reporter. Troy was definitely an affectionate dog. I almost started laughing until Richard glared at me and I studied the plastic plant in the corner some more.

The interview went well and the reporter seemed fascinated with their tales. The only problem was he struggled to understand Richard's tricky speech and he kept looking at me to explain. Since my wounds were still fresh from my recent blunder in this area, I knew better than to speak for Richard like he wasn't in the room. That was when I learned the strategy I employed for years when dealing with people who tried to take the shortcut and talk to me instead of Richard.

I refused to take my eyes off my boss.

I felt rude not to acknowledge the reporter, especially since he was trying to put Richard on the news, yet I knew how it angered Richard to be bypassed, and I couldn't blame him. I would've felt the same. There was nothing wrong with Richard's intellect; the door was just stuck.

Eventually, either Richard gave me the green light to clarify one of his answers (though I was still adjusting to his slurred speech, too), or the reporter had no choice but to turn back to Richard since I wouldn't look at him. Later, Richard suggested I tell people at the outset of a conversation they should direct all questions to him and not to me, which was good advice.

Near the end of the interview, the reporter asked Michael if he was proud of his dad for overcoming adversity and always being there for him. Michael looked down for a few moments before finally shrugging and answering, "Yeah. I mean, he's just my dad." As I drove home, I realized that was probably the best answer Michael could've given and the one most coveted by Richard—not to be known for his physical challenge, but simply a dad with a good sense of humor and a cute dog who liked to walk his son home from school.

CHAPTER THREE

The Elephant Awakens

Somehow, he passed.

By the grace of God, two late nights, and a gallon of coffee, we plowed our way through Richard's seventeen-page sermon on the nature of unconditional forgiveness, submitting it eighty-six minutes before the deadline. Because his professor had to turn in his grades soon, we didn't have to wait long to learn our fate. Richard received an "A" and passed his class by the width of a fingernail.

As if that triumph wasn't enough to celebrate, Richard and Michael's story aired on TV the following week. It was raining good news. Richard couldn't stop smiling. He invited over a few friends from church for a viewing party. The segment aired at the end of the news broadcast and was put together well, though my fifteen minutes of fame had to wait since I was excluded from the final cut (I needed a good agent). I could tell Richard was proud and pleased as everyone congratulated Michael and him. It was the happiest I'd seen Richard yet, and it seemed like he'd finally entered a peaceful, satisfying period of life after so many years of struggle.

Until the next day when he started bawling.

I had no idea what was wrong or how to console him or if I should leave him alone to collect himself. I stood lost in the middle of his living room watching Troy climb onto Richard's lap to lick his face. It was actually quite poignant. Just as I began backing out of the room to let the two of them hug it out, Richard blubbered, "Wait…wait."

I froze, hoping he might forget I was there if I stayed silent and motionless. Then he waved me over, and the only thing racing through my mind was, *Please don't hug me. I'm not Troy. Hands off!* Aside from my mom, my family had never endorsed displays of affection. Or encouragement. Or acknowledgment, for that matter. My three highly competitive older brothers, dad, and I were all obsessed with beating each other at anything, and a pat on the back, much less a hug with tears, simply didn't happen. That poor sap would've been heckled mercilessly for a decade. Most of the time, we pretended not to know each other in public.

We were very enlightened and mature.

On top of that, I was extremely quiet and shy, so Richard, an extroverted, affectionate, emotionally accessible man whose love languages clearly included physical contact, was my antithesis. My hands began trembling as I approached him. What did he want from me that able service dog Troy Aikman couldn't offer? I was a leftover sardine compared to Troy in this department.

Richard pointed to the couch for me to sit down, and I practically shrieked, "Yes, sir." Whatever it was, we could work through it together from a safe, healthy distance with no touching. He slowly inched his chair into the center of the room and turned so he was facing me. He took a moment to compose himself. I waited patiently. I was in no hurry to dig into this. Something told me it was going to be heavy with no easy solution. I considered offering to fetch him some sweet tea, always a hit, yet kept quiet.

Finally, Richard calmed down and looked at me, while gently petting Troy on his head as he sat dutifully beside the wheelchair. Richard then said two words that forever changed our lives: "I'm lonely."

I almost blurted, *Don't look at me.* I didn't know what he had in mind, but this definitely wasn't in our contract. I managed to restrain myself long enough to hear him out. He said, "I miss being married...but I don't miss my ex-wife." He started chuckling and coughing, and I grabbed his giant cup for him to drink. I sat back down, and he continued, "I need a companion, somebody to talk to. Somebody who loves me for me." He started to say something else, but his crying resumed, and Troy immediately climbed up on his chair. I sat with my hands clasped in my lap, unsure of what to do. I supposed a comforting pat on the back was in order, but again, how did one go about that?

After a few moments, Troy climbed down, as Richard said, "And Michael needs a mom. He's so young. His own mom's a train wreck." I couldn't help but laugh out loud. I wasn't sure if that was appropriate, yet thankfully, Richard laughed, too.

"Well, what about at church?" I suggested. "Maybe there's somebody nice there you could meet." I felt like a pathetic knockoff version of Dear Abby.

Richard shook his head and explained, "They're all married. Or young."

I frantically tried to think of another possible solution before he started crying again, though this wasn't my field of expertise. All I could come up with was, "Maybe you'll meet someone in the community. Or through a friend."

"Nobody knows no one," he grumbled dismissively. He was careening toward the abyss. I needed to pull him back before it was too late. I scratched my head and looked around, desperately trying to think of what he could do. And then I saw his computer.

"Hey, Richard, have you ever thought about online dating?" I asked hopefully.

There was a stigma attached to dating sites when they'd first appeared that they were only for the weirdest, most unattractive, and socially inept losers who couldn't meet people in the "real" world. But now public perception had shifted to the more accurate view that not everyone was nineteen with plenty of years and options to bump into their soulmate. For a thirty-eight-year-old divorced mother of two, one of the best avenues available to find someone willing and able to step into her world was the Internet. Richard was looking for a rare woman who could meet his unique, incessant needs while feeling completely content. There wasn't one of these ladies in every corner drugstore. We needed the widest possible perimeter for our search: the world.

At first, Richard didn't respond, yet he also didn't reject it. I could tell he was on the train to Funk Town and didn't want to raise his hopes, but this idea had undeniable potential. He held out as long as he could, until finally he sighed and said, "What do I have to lose?"

We were on. I sat down at his computer and began our quest to find Richard a new wife. If I'd stopped for two seconds to think about how daunting the task was, I probably would've scrapped the idea and taken Richard for ice cream to distract him. Not only was I attempting to help guide him to a master's degree and, ultimately, a job in the community, which would take years of diligent work, but now we were going to create a new family for him. It was the toughest challenge I'd ever undertaken, and not typical for me at all. I tended to avoid responsibility so I could remain focused on my own passions and pursuits. Yet after many years of this, maybe I was ready for something else. Something more. I needed to put somebody else first for a change. The greatest rewards were given away, and I wanted to try that approach. I wanted to help Richard, or at least give it my best shot. I really didn't know if we could pull it off, but like Richard said, we could try. I was motivated and optimistic, and he'd stopped crying. It was a step in the right direction.

Admittedly, it felt good to help him. When we'd found out he passed his class, it was a lot more fulfilling than I'd anticipated. Even though I was working closer to thirty hours a week while still getting paid for only ten, I didn't feel cheated or used. I felt needed. I wasn't just another warm body to fill a position, I was indispensable. That was a job perk not easily matched.

I quickly realized that my official title of tutor only scratched the surface. We worked on Richard's new class most days, yet I also typed emails for him, helped with phone calls, made him meals, fed him, occasionally changed his shirt if he spilled food or tea on it, and accompanied him on errands. Basically, I was his assistant. At first, it bothered me that we were doing so many other things unrelated to schoolwork, but as time passed, I cherished the variety. Each day was broken up into thirds: a few hours on classwork, a few hours on calls and letters, and a few hours out in the community. It made the day fly by much faster than if I'd merely sat in front of his computer for eight hours. It was another unforeseen job benefit and a daily reminder of how much I didn't know.

There was no shortage of reminders.

When I'd first returned to Fort Worth, my top priority was to move my roommate, Bryan, and myself out of his parents' house. They were nice, considerate, and generous people, but I wanted our own space. We looked at several apartments yet didn't take the plunge. If we had, we would've been evicted after the first month or two. We simply couldn't afford it, but living with Bryan's folks turned out to be a blessing in disguise. Not only did it permit me to help Richard for less pay, it also allowed Bryan to remain with his parents, especially his mom with whom he was very close. Bryan had struggled with depression, manic mood swings, intense anxieties bordering on panic attacks, and severe ADHD for nearly twenty years. He'd been suicidal, gotten arrested, and slept in his car many nights. He was now on medication, going to counseling, back in graduate school, and trying to get his life together. Living with his folks was exactly where we needed to be, yet I'd been convinced of the opposite.

Bryan and I had also started a band in Dallas with a tremendous female vocalist. Before Bryan found her, I was certain we needed to limit our search to Fort Worth because of the distance to Dallas. Yet when he played me some of her recordings, and then I heard her in person, Dallas seemed like a block away.

Everything I'd been sure of was dead wrong, and the last thing I wanted turned out to be the best. My lack of foresight and judgment astounded me. But rather than beat myself up on a daily basis, I decided to concentrate on the flipside of the coin: At least I'd remained open-minded. If I hadn't, I would've missed out on it all.

This was the attitude I adopted for my job with Richard and for life in general. I even said a prayer on my way to work each morning that I was willing to do whatever God wanted just as long as He made it clear to me, because otherwise I'd miss it. I needed it spelled out in large, *crystal*-clear capital letters. With blinking lights and fireworks. And a foghorn. Of course, I could've just used George Costanza's method on *Seinfeld* and done the opposite of my natural inclination. That sounded foolproof.

Though, the first time Richard asked me to help him defecate, I started reevaluating my gut instinct's accuracy.

I'd been lucky my first few weeks with him—no pooping on my watch. I felt like I was a free man living behind enemy lines. I was on borrowed time and I knew it. One day, the elephant napping in the room was going to need to go potty, and I was thoroughly unprepared for it.

Part of why I'd dodged the bullet for this long was Richard didn't want to waste our time together relieving himself. He needed my help getting schoolwork and paperwork done. He could go to the bathroom later. He was also being incredibly considerate of my germaphobia, of which he was well aware. He always tried to have a bowel movement in the morning before I arrived, or he simply held it until I left. It was one of the most selfless things anyone had ever done for me.

Unfortunately, that didn't make this any easier.

We were both sitting in front of his computer. He was looking at me, waiting for my response to his request, while I scanned the screen for a portal to another galaxy. Finally, I glanced at him and the need was obvious: Richard had *I GOTTA GO* tattooed across his anguished face. There was no way out, and besides, this was my job. I'd signed up. He was under my care until the night shift arrived.

Maybe it won't be so bad, I reassured myself as we relocated to Richard's bedroom. *We'll laugh about it...it'll be fun.* I was panicking and desperate. His room appeared twice as small as usual. I wanted to wash my hands and we hadn't even done anything yet.

That reminded me—gloves! "Hey, Richard, uh…do you happen to have some…gloves I could wear?" I hoped this wouldn't offend him, but at the moment, I was far more concerned with not fainting.

He smiled and said, "You want two pair?"

That sounded like a splendid idea. Did he have plenty to spare? I wondered if I could stretch them over my entire body. I needed a Hazmat suit.

I found the gloves in a bottom cabinet in his bathroom and squeezed my hands into two pairs. When I turned around, Richard pointed to another cabinet. When I opened it, I discovered a box of surgical masks. I smiled and nodded, and he started laughing. It was a very thoughtful gesture, and I happily slipped one on. "Just hurry up before I go in my pants," he cracked. I looked like I was ready to perform open-heart surgery.

As he positioned his wheelchair underneath the lift and I lowered the bar with the three straps, he asked, "You okay to wipe?"

I was still coming to grips with what was about to happen; I really didn't need him to spell it out. Yet it got worse.

He looked up at me and specified, just in case there was any confusion, "In the hole."

I almost passed out. *He didn't just say that, did he?* My head felt hot and my mouth began watering like I was about to vomit.

I didn't respond, I simply gritted my teeth and tried to get through it as quickly as I could. After I unfastened his ankle bands that kept his feet from sliding off his footrests, and then removed his shoes, he told me to take off his dress shirt to get it out of the way. Next, he instructed me to put only the strap under his arms and hook it to the bar, raise him enough to slide off his pants, and then lower him back down into his chair and place the other two straps around his bare thighs and fasten them to the bar. Richard didn't wear underwear because he had a condom catheter attached from his penis to a urine bag strapped to his left ankle. Suddenly, I was face to face with a naked man. Things were spiraling wildly out of control. I'd understood I'd have to remove his pants for him to be able to use the bathroom, yet reality left nothing to the imagination. I literally closed my eyes for a moment trying to picture the beach.

Then I had to pull the condom catheter off his penis and unsnap the urine bag from his ankle. I was starting to have an out-of-body experience and could see myself reaching toward his private parts as I frantically tried to wave myself off from above. *ABORT! ABORT!* I screamed from the ceiling, to no avail. I hustled to the bathroom and emptied the urine bag in the toilet, and then placed the bag and catheter on the end of his bed, reminding myself never to touch that corner of his bedspread again.

Richard was now ready for takeoff. For weeks afterward, I couldn't erase the image of a naked Richard flying through the air on his lift toward the toilet. I watched a different movie every night to bury the memory as deeply as possible. Nothing worked.

The final hurdle of the operation was by far the toughest, and at that point, my knees were wobbly. I felt like a dazed boxer in the last round of a slugfest. Couldn't Troy take it from here? He was wisely staying out of this. I raised Richard off the toilet and moved him in position to wipe him. I really wished I had put on a third pair of gloves. I grabbed a wad of toilet paper as thick as a phone book and tried to steady myself. I was sweating through my mask. His small bathroom felt like it was on fire. Could the lights have been any brighter? I wanted to turn them off so I couldn't see what was happening. To his credit, poor Richard just hung there on his lift waiting for me to pull it together. He didn't complain or sigh or anything. He knew he was breaking in a pitiful rookie.

There was no way out except in, so I took my softball of toilet paper and did my duty. Between the second and third wipe, the room started spinning and I had to put my left hand on the wall to prop myself up. I didn't think I was going to make it. If we waited long enough, the night attendant would arrive and she could finish. Of course, that was in three hours. Maybe Richard would fall asleep up there and we could just ride it out.

I shook my head and refocused on the job at hand. I needed to finish and put him back in his chair. It wasn't safe or comfortable for him to be suspended in the air this long. I wiped two more times before the mission was successful, and then dressed and returned Richard to his chair as expeditiously as I could.

Then I threw away my gloves and mask, and scrubbed my hands for three minutes.

Richard thanked me and smiled, and asked, "Did you survive?"

I wasn't sure. I was soaked with sweat and felt like I needed a shot of whiskey. That was more physical contact than I had with myself. I didn't think I could ever get used to it, and I was concerned that it would become a regular occurrence now that we'd tamed the elephant. To this point, working for Richard wasn't as bad as I'd projected and I didn't dread going to work. But if we started taking daily trips to the bathroom, I thought I might have to quit.

Of course, I didn't say this. It wasn't fair or right to present Richard with the ultimatum, *Stop pooping or else.* I felt pretty evil just thinking it. Yet it was my attitude and I didn't know if it would change. I hoped time would take care of the matter, either allowing me to grow used to accommodating all of Richard's needs or spacing enough distance between crises so it wasn't overwhelming. I still felt like I wasn't exactly cut out for this line of work. But Richard liked me, and as hard as I resisted, he was wiggling his way into my world full-time. I wasn't even looking for other jobs anymore. He took up most of my week, and besides, East Gourmet Buffet had just started serving chocolate mousse on their dessert table. Time was already paying dividends.

"Yeah, I made it," I answered Richard, with a thumbs-up for reassurance.

"You wanna switch to mornings?" he joked with an even wider grin.

I waved my hand and shook my head. "No, thank you." I was on the right shift, for more reasons than I could've guessed.

CHAPTER FOUR

Protector of the Disheartened

The next month with Richard felt more like *Love Connection* than tutoring. In fact, as our online search progressed, it became quite clear that Richard was far more interested in hunting for possible matches than studying hermeneutics. I couldn't blame him. It was a lot more exciting trying to find the love of his life than reading textbooks. Richard had a program on his computer that read books for him while highlighting each word (it helped reinforce the text to people with reading and writing difficulties to hear it read aloud while seeing the words), and after two hours of listening to that droning automated voice (I called it Computer Lady), I was ready for us to troll dating sites, too.

Richard picked a Christian site and signed up for a year. He was in it to win it. After two weeks, he made a friend and they "chatted" a bit, but nothing serious. Then Della entered our lives. She'd been on the site for only a few days, yet she appreciated Richard's testimony we'd posted, and she wrote him a letter. Upon finishing reading her letter, Richard looked at me and said, "She's the one." I assumed he meant the one with whom he wanted to focus communicating, but he had other ideas. He was already planning their lives together.

Della lived in Tennessee, and she really didn't think it'd go anywhere, primarily because of the distance between them. Yet she still enjoyed talking with Richard. At least once a week, he called her in the evening using an operator at the relay service center who helped translate anything Della couldn't understand. Richard said he didn't want to take up our time during the day with personal calls, though I had a hunch it had more to do with his self-consciousness, which I completely understood. One of the scariest things I'd ever attempted was to call a girl, so whatever he needed to do for confidence was totally justified.

We wrote Della letters a few times a week, and one day while dictating, Richard said, "You should do this."

"Huh? Do what?" I replied, though I suspected what he was talking about.

He just pointed at the computer screen and smiled.

"Build computers?" I joked, stalling. "I don't think I'd have the time."

He touched his joystick to make his chair recline all the way back, and he said, "Pull me up, funny man." Every now and then, Richard needed to be readjusted in his chair because he gradually slid out of a comfortable position throughout the day. I jumped up, happy to help steer us away from the previous topic. After I unsnapped his ankle bands, I stood behind his head, which was down around my waist, and slipped my hands under his armpits. Then on the count of three, I pulled him toward me, allowing him to sit straighter and higher. He raised his chair back upright, and said, "Thanks." As I was fastening his ankle bands, he said, "Well?"

"What?" I asked, unable to play dumb without grinning.

He started laughing and said, "Why don't you try it, too?" He waited a beat and added, "We could double date." Harder laughing accompanied by inevitable coughing ensued.

I sat down and shook my head. "What makes you think I'm looking for a serious relationship? You think I'm ready for that?" I was a mostly unsuccessful writer and musician, had lived in nine states in the past fifteen years, didn't even have my own place, and was now making part-time pay. I wasn't exactly Prince Charming material.

"You've seen my car, and that's as good as it gets."

Richard pulled closer to me, as I braced for impact. I was sure a hug was coming. But he merely said, "You think that's what girls care about?"

I nodded, and replied, "Uh, yeah, I think it's crossed their minds. I know it has mine."

"What about somebody nice to talk to?" When I didn't respond, he pointed his crooked right index finger at me and said, "Like you."

I smiled, knowing his heart was in the right place. I'd actually come to expect it from him. He rarely missed an opportunity to encourage me. I wondered if it was a reaction to a lifetime of neglect and mistreatment, but Richard couldn't stand seeing me, or anyone, disheartened. He was all too familiar with the feeling and now sat blocking the entrance. I found it incredibly ironic that a man slighted so much in life was one of the biggest encouragers I'd met. He wasn't immune to melancholy, as his meltdown over being single demonstrated, yet he didn't overindulge in self-pity. Feeling sorry for himself was a bottomless hole Richard couldn't afford to dig, because there was no one else to help shovel him out.

Yet despite his good intentions, I thought his position on this particular matter was overly optimistic. I said, "That's important, too, but the rest of the package matters."

He didn't say anything for a few moments, a habit of his I'd come to admire. He tried to process everything before unleashing a comment, something most embraced as critical yet few actually did. His face grew more serious, and the advice he picked was something my mother used to say when I was growing up: "Don't borrow trouble." I smiled upon hearing these familiar words, and he added, "Let the girl make up her own mind."

It was hard to argue with that, yet it was also difficult to recognize self-worth when tallied in public. The fruits of my labor didn't add up to an attractive portfolio measured against the world's paradigm of success, and the road less traveled I'd taken so eagerly and confidently years ago didn't appear to offer any remaining on-ramps to the freeway. It felt like I was on a moving walkway at the airport unable to slow down or change direction; I could only wave like a tourist to all that had once blocked the view. It was a sobering, frightening realization, one I'd known for some time yet kept at arm's length. I felt helpless, angry, and pretty much alone.

When I looked over at Richard, he was smiling like we were the two luckiest blokes alive. "Am I right?" he asked exuberantly. "Huh?"

Mr. Persistent, protector of the disheartened. I shook my head and finally cracked a smile. It was hard to argue with him.

The road less traveled hadn't begun with Bryan, but he definitely helped gather snacks for the road trip. We'd known each other for fourteen years, going back to a chance encounter at the same seminary he now attended. I'd just started classes, having graduated college a few months before with the intent of becoming Ernest Hemingway. I was one of the only students with long hair, which peaked Bryan's interest since he was a fan of alternative music and thought I might be, too (most of our schoolmates at the conservative seminary weren't big into grunge). That was actually his greeting when he'd first spotted me in the school library: "Hey, do you like alternative music?" I glanced behind me hoping to find the person he was addressing. I was on my own.

Bryan was six feet, four inches and thin, with blond hair and a small hoop earring in his left ear. Was he accusing me of violating the school's music policy? He wasn't dressed like campus security. Surely, they didn't allow earrings on the force. Was he attempting to make a citizen's arrest? I considered answering in Spanish to throw him off my scent, but I only remembered a few words and *No sé* would get me only so far. If he spoke Spanish, my cover was blown. Finally, I shrugged and answered, "I guess."

That was all he needed. With his foot in the door, Bryan provided me with a complete rundown of his favorite alternative bands, songs, videos, and magazines. He described his acoustic and electric guitars, amp, and preferred tuner. Occasionally, I inserted a "Cool" or "Me, too" to keep the spotlight on him while I picked the best excuse to disappear.

He seemed like a nice guy, just talkative, and I wasn't in the mood for conversation. Ever. I despised talking on the phone and avoided interaction in person. Sometimes, I played a game of how long I could go without speaking to anyone. Three weeks was my record. I was a bit anti-social.

However, Bryan, like Richard, was persistent and remained undeterred despite my abrupt exit from the library. Over the next three weeks, he chased me down on campus numerous times until I ran out of bushes to duck behind. He was like a bulldog that wouldn't let go. Eventually, I gave in and we became friends. But he wasn't done with me yet.

He liked a few of the essays I'd written and he kept hounding me to try writing songs. He wanted to jam. I was reluctant since I couldn't play an instrument and didn't care much for poetry, but the bulldog was dug in for the long haul.

The result was I took up piano and guitar, we started a band with my roommate, Tripp, and after I graduated, we all moved to Atlanta where Tripp's family lived. Tripp's childhood friend, Winn, became our singer, and a seasoned musician named Scott answered our ad in the paper for a drummer. For the next four years, we played gigs in the Southeast, recorded demos, printed band shirts, rehearsed tirelessly, worked part-time jobs, scraped pennies together for rent, ate a lot of peanut butter sandwiches, sweated countless hours in our van, and then broke up. The band had run its course, or maybe we needed a break. Unfortunately, endings often masqueraded as pauses. Tripp got married, I moved to South Florida to live with old friends, and Bryan went off the deep end. The band ended right around the time Bryan's relationship with his girlfriend fizzled and his side business installing mini-blinds sank him deeper in debt than he already was. The coalescence of these blows was more than his chemical imbalance could stand, so he turned to a brief life of crime for a quick score to fix all.

Larceny wasn't exactly a perfect fit for Bryan.

One night, he decided to break into the Piggly Wiggly, yet it wasn't until he climbed on top of the store with his bag of tools that he realized he'd forgotten his huge crowbar down in his truck. He sat on the roof berating himself for a minute or two before scampering all the way back down to retrieve it. Later, he stole a tractor-trailer with the intent of filling it with ATMs he collected around town, but unfortunately, he rear-ended a car and then couldn't crack open any of the ATMs. Finally, he decided to flee to Miami in hopes of networking with the Mafia. When those coveted doors failed to open, he ran out of money and decided to fish for food while crashing on the beach. But he was arrested stealing bait before he could live off the land, halting his crime spree.

Bryan managed to avoid major jail time and moved back in with his folks in Fort Worth. We didn't see each other for three years until I had the notion to set a novel on the border to Mexico and picked tiny Port Isabel, just across the bridge from South Padre Island, as home. Bryan was up for a new adventure and moved down, and for the first year or so, life was fairly uneventful. He was on medication, worked at a dive shop, and seemed to be enjoying himself. Yet, once again, he started a side business, this time in web design, and fell so far behind in orders that he panicked and disappeared. When three days passed without word, I feared he was either arrested or dead. The next morning, a call from the police station in Brownsville confirmed my suspicions—he'd been arrested for shoplifting. When I bailed him out, he didn't say a word on the ride back to our apartment. Finally, I asked, "What'd you steal?"

"Software," he mumbled, looking out the window as I pulled into our parking lot. "From Best Buy."

"What'd you need that for?"

At first, he didn't answer. Then as I parked, he said, "I didn't, not really. I just wanted it. So I took it." I tried to pick the response that might set him off the least, but before I chose, he muttered, "Wanted to be in control for once."

And that was it. He didn't say much more the rest of the week as we packed and headed back to his parents' house in Fort Worth. I felt guilty dumping him on his folks as I hightailed it out of town. I didn't know what else to do for him, and I really didn't want him to die on my watch. He needed more help than I could give, or at least that was what I told myself as I left.

I didn't see Bryan again for five years, but I often thought about what he said regarding being in control. It seemed his extreme mood swings, ADHD, depression, and major insecurities left him stuck on an endless roller coaster of emotions. He was convinced he was powerless over his own life, like he had no say in his future, dreams, career, success, romance, or even feelings. It was all up to somebody else, or nobody, but certainly not him. Whether he was adrift forsaken by God or simply incapable of steering straight on his own, he didn't know and increasingly didn't care. The only thing he knew for certain was he was a screw-up, a failure, and that he "sucked at life," as he'd declared more than once. He had command over nothing, and the harder he grasped at what he most wanted, the more he fumbled it. So he stole things, anything, just to get his hands on something tangible that was his and couldn't be lost at the last second. He stole to accomplish a feat, to see it through to the end without giving in.

Of course, shoplifting guaranteed his self-fulfilling prophecy that he'd never emerge from the undertow. Ironically, the liberating sense of command flooding his system as he safely exited a grocery store with power bars and cookies stuffed down his extra baggy pants was the most potent form of sabotage he employed. Even in his rebellion against himself, he couldn't pronounce victory without strings attached.

Perhaps after years of being the victim, Bryan depended on the role as his identity and alibi for not holding it together. If he wasn't emotionally unstable, where was the irrefutable progress that could be proudly displayed to relatives at holiday meals? Where was the normalcy, the dependability? His role built a trapdoor for him to slip through just when a corner might be turned.

As much as he worried and exhausted me, I still missed Bryan and kept in touch with him over the next five years. I also missed playing music in a band, having merely written and recorded songs on my own since we all went our separate ways in Atlanta. When I told Bryan I was interested in forming a new group, he immediately started making lists of potential names, clubs we could play in Dallas, and avenues for finding a singer. He actually sounded a lot like he did when we'd first met in the school library.

It didn't take him long to track down Manya, an incredible singer in Dallas who was open to practicing with us. I was living in Raleigh at the time working odd jobs while writing another book and more songs. I'd moved around a lot since Atlanta, writing and submitting work while collecting a duffel bag full of rejection letters. Yet when I heard the recordings Bryan sent, I knew it was time to pack once more.

Six weeks later, I knocked on Richard's front door.

CHAPTER FIVE

GO

After five months with Richard, I was working forty hours a week while getting paid for twenty-five. Things weren't perfect, but they were slowly leveling out. His other two attendants had been with him longer, though one had started just two months before I. The other had been with Richard off and on for two and a half years, so I was still last on the totem pole. His CLASS program allotted Richard only so many attendant hours per week, which created a tacit rule with his staff that time was money. Richard wasn't about to yank pay out of his oldest attendant's pocket for some new hire who might quit next month. If I wanted more cash, I had to put in the time, but we were getting there.

During my months with Richard, one realization I'd been forced to accept, practically at gunpoint, was the stark contrast between insecurities and inhibitions. Richard had plenty of insecurities about his slurred speech, the respect of his peers, his value to the community, his effectiveness as a father, and on and on. He was a big ball of self-doubt.

But he had zero inhibitions.

Zilch.

It didn't matter where we were or what was happening around us, Richard never hesitated to make himself right at home. He did things I wouldn't have tried if I'd been all by myself. But to Richard, he *was* by himself. He didn't seem to notice, or certainly mind, if he was in the middle of a crowded room. He did what he had to do to get comfortable, probably because he was in pain most of the time. Either his back ached, his bottom was peppered with saddle sores from sitting in his wheelchair all day, his migraines tag-teamed him, or his ankles and feet were swollen from tendinitis. He didn't have time to worry about what others thought. When it came to his health, spectators were at the back of a very long line.

This truth was pounded home to me the first time we visited the Food Stamps Office in Fort Worth. There had been a mix-up with Richard's renewal form, and though he'd long since turned in his change of address before moving to Wheaton Street, the only thing he received in the mail from the F.S.O. was a voter registration card. His food stamps had now been cut off, so we went down to Ground Zero to battle it out.

Disneyland it was not. Or even Newfoundland. Or Cleveland.

When we walked in, I wasn't sure what the legal room capacity was, but I hoped nobody started any fires. Three lines stretched from the door to the available windows currently open to customers (two were closed). There were also seven rows of folks sitting and waiting, presumably to be called back for a face-to-face with someone possessing the requisite clout to untangle their thickets of red tape. People were packed in that room like knickknacks in a junk drawer. Many I dared examine close enough were sweating, as the air conditioner was either broken or a cost-cutting casualty. Nobody looked happy to be there. I knew I wasn't. Little kids darted around; the angry, loud women behind the windows kept hollering "*Next*" or various numbers like we were waiting for pastrami in a deli; at least three men milling about looked and smelled drunk; two young women with sleeve tattoos were arguing in the back corner about hair extensions (as best I could tell); several babies cried continuously until I was ready to nurse them; the tall, lanky man ahead of us in line clutched his pack of cigarettes like they were his heart pills in case he collapsed; and a middle-aged man and woman were curled up on their chairs snoring loudly. It was a circus. One older man in the first row finally snapped and yelled, "I'm 'bout sick and tired of sittin' up in here! Somebody better call my number right now!!" I started nodding in case he glanced my way looking for solidarity. I had his back.

We waited in line a good forty minutes *just to get a number.* Then the real waiting began, but unfortunately, there hadn't been an empty seat since the lights first flicked on that morning. I found a pole to lean against, as Richard parked beside me. I took turns fanning us both with our number. I scanned behind me to see if there were any potential pickpocket threats, and when I looked back at Richard, he was gone. How could he move anywhere in that crawl space? How could I lose him here? I stood on my tiptoes searching the far wall for him but couldn't find him. I started weaving my way through the lines, quietly calling his name like he'd wandered off during story time in the library, until I came upon him. He was hard to miss.

There, in front of Fort Worth's finest, with every disgruntled face and bleary eye on him, Richard reclined his chair until he was lying horizontally like it was time for bed. And go to sleep was precisely what he did. He closed his eyes, and within a matter of ninety seconds, started snoring louder than the middle-aged couple balled up on their chairs. The deafening noise, curious crowd of onlookers, uncertainty of his eligibility for food stamps, heat—nothing fazed Richard. He was tired and his body needed rest, so it was naptime. I couldn't move him out of the way because he was fully reclined and I would've had to straighten him first. Besides, he didn't seem bothered at all by his location.

He slept for an hour and a half until I woke him because our number had finally been shrieked. I was in awe of his sleeping prowess. How did he do it? What was his secret? He'd slept in the middle of a roadside carnival. People had actually bumped him as they trudged by. I'd stood guard the best I could, yet short of draping my body across his, it was impossible to shield him from all contact since he was napping on a subway platform during rush hour.

As a stocky woman with arm-wrestler forearms held the door open for us to go kneel before the food stamp king's throne, I envied Richard's lack of inhibitions. It must've been a liberating way to go through life. Ironically, he probably experienced more freedom on a daily basis in his wheelchair than I did stumbling around paranoid about what others thought. In fact, it didn't seem like too many of the raucous throng we were leaving worried a whole lot about their fellow man's opinion. They simply did what they wanted without wasting a second on appearances. If somebody had an issue, take a number. They were busy being themselves. Richard was like that. He felt more comfortable in his own skin than I, and as we made our way down the hall to our meeting, I realized that out of the entire cast of kooky characters we'd just met, I was the weird one in the room.

For Thanksgiving, Richard decided turkey and stuffing weren't enough. It was time to take his relationship with Della to the next level. The great face-to-face meeting had arrived.

I felt even more nervous than Richard. What if Della didn't

like him in person? It had taken me some time to come around to his subtle charms. Richard himself liked to joke that he was "an acquired taste." What if she took one look at him and bailed? His self-esteem already dragged behind him. If she broke it off, he might not mend. There were many gloomy days in Funk Town ahead of us if this turned sour.

I counseled caution to buy us time. "What would it hurt to get to know her a little more?" I tossed out innocently, pleading inside. "Lay a strong foundation. And remember, absence makes the heart grow fonder." I was hurling every cliché I knew.

"Not the brown," Richard merely answered, as I deliberately packed the wrong dress pants in his suitcase. "The blue. You color blind?" he teased.

Yes, if that was what it took.

"Is she excited or nervous?" I asked, curious if he knew for certain. They'd spoken on the phone last night and finalized their plans. She was having Thanksgiving dinner with her family and he was invited to come. Now, it wasn't entirely clear *who* had done the inviting. He said he told Della he would come, yet I didn't know if that was in response to her request or if he'd invited himself. I had my suspicions. It was hard to know for sure because Richard had a way of imposing his will without insisting. His persistence, determination, and excitement left little room for alternative plans. There was one way to proceed and it was the route he happened to favor and everybody was glad to be on board helping out.

I supposed, in the end, our own preferences felt fairly trivial compared to Richard's needs and the chance to serve him in some small way. However noble our intentions, though, there was usually a small dash of selfishness mixed in, as there was no denying it made us all feel better to help him.

I really didn't feel like pressing the issue of whether he was about to descend on Della and her family before she was ready to see him. He didn't need to hear negativity right now. He was under enough pressure, and it was a moot point anyway. His tickets were bought, his bags almost packed, and he and Michael and Troy were flying to Manchester, Tennessee, tomorrow evening. All we could do now was hope for the best with infinite optimism.

That was when he told me. It literally felt like the wind got knocked out of me.

He wasn't just going to Manchester to see Della, eat a bunch of food, spill lots of gravy on his bib, and take a nap in the middle of everyone. He had other intentions. Major ones. My only response was, "Say that again."

He smiled and razzed, "Now you're blind and deaf?"

Again, if that was what it took.

He repeated once more for the blind, deaf, and dumbfounded in the room, "I'm gonna propose to Della."

"Marriage?"

"What else?"

I could think of a few suggestions. Horseshoes? A double feature? Was it too late to take him out for ice cream and forget this online dating business? I wasn't sure how this would go over, but I had to say it: "Richard, you haven't even met her in person. Don't you think you're rushing things a bit?"

He laughed like I was doing a stand-up routine. He said, "When you know, you know."

I wanted to point out several historical examples of leaders who'd been absolutely certain they were doing the right thing and weren't even close. Hitler came to mind. Yet rather than detour into World War II, I kept the focus on the crisis at hand. "Just remember one thing," I emphasized. "You and Della have both been married before. She might not be as anxious to dive into another marriage as you. You should take it slow. Don't risk scaring her off."

Unfortunately, Richard knew only one speed—GO—and he was in gear. I wasn't even sure he heard me. It reminded me of my older brother, David, who had struggled with drugs when he was a teenager. It took him almost ten years to get clean, but when he finally went off to college in his mid-twenties, he did his four-year degree in three years. When I asked why, he said he had lots of time to make up. It seemed Richard wanted to win back lost time, too, as fast as possible. He wanted to prove everyone wrong and grab the dream before it slithered away. His future was now, and I couldn't blame him. I just didn't want to see his spirit crushed.

The next day was phase one of Richard's Master Plan. He and Troy and I headed to the nearby mall to secure an engagement ring. Of course, Richard cut a deal with the manager of the jewelry store for a price reduction on his chosen ring. He was a master salesman and could smile his way into a discount with anyone. When it was time to pay, Richard had Troy clutch his wallet in his mouth and drop it on the counter, and then as we exited the store, Troy carried the bag with his teeth. I was a little nervous Troy might get excited and chomp down on the contents, yet Richard wasn't concerned.

We spent the day taking care of last-minute preparations for his trip, as well as doing a little schoolwork. He was slogging his way through Spiritual Formation and Discipleship Ministries, his two classes during the current eight-week session. Every eight weeks we did two more, though Richard had wisely started with just one class to get used to the coursework. I was looking forward to the Christmas break when the school train finally pulled into the station for a rest. We'd survived two more classes and were now pushing through our fourth and fifth since I began. The pressure was far greater than I'd anticipated. I wanted Richard to learn as much as possible and improve his study techniques and writing abilities, yet we also had to finish by the deadlines. Weeks rolled by as we crept through textbooks listening to Computer Lady torture us, and when we looked up, a week remained in the session before all assignments had to be submitted. The last few days of each class were a mad dash to the finish line, with many late nights and nerve-wracking exams. Richard passed every course, though, and the dream of earning a master's degree was still alive.

I couldn't afford to fly with Richard to Tennessee, but at least he had Michael and Troy. Plus, Bryan was battling through his first semester back at seminary, so I wanted to make sure he didn't short-circuit under pressure. I seemed to be his security blanket, which made me feel valuable but also torn because I knew Richard could've used my help, too. I was extremely concerned Richard's Master Plan wouldn't turn out quite the way he envisioned. Plots were rarely executed without hiccups. I actually told him that right before I left and his evening attendant arrived to prepare him for a good night's rest for his early-morning flight. I said, "Just remember, you may not land on the runway, but a field will do nicely." He looked up at me, horrified, and I realized what I'd said. "Not your *flight*—I don't mean your flight. Figuratively speaking. Your *plan.* I mean your plan might not work out perfectly, but it'll still be fine. Just stay open-minded. Okay?"

He smiled and laughed like everything was a done deal. "Happy Thanksgiving," was all he said as I pulled out my keys to leave. *I hope it is,* I thought. *I hope it is.*

CHAPTER SIX

A Second Chance for Three

The best-laid plans…

Richard's morning attendant had an unexpected emergency and couldn't come, so a nearby volunteer was pressed into service to bathe and dress him for his trip. I lived too far away to make it in time, and I didn't know his morning routine anyway. For some odd reason, the volunteer thought Steve Urkel's look would win over Della, so when Richard got off the plane to meet her, his dress shirt was tucked deeply into his pants, while his trousers were hiked up near his armpits. All he was missing was the huge glasses.

As if that wasn't enough of a fashion statement, Richard dyed the gray in his hair brown. He desperately wanted to impress Della.

I later asked why he'd dyed his hair, and he simply answered, "Why not? Makes me feel good."

I couldn't argue with that.

Then he confessed, in an admirable show of honesty, "I wanted to look younger."

Didn't we all.

Della wasn't sure what to make of him. He was stuffed in an airport wheelchair, his dyed hair poking out of what was left of his shirt—it looked like his pants were the tide rising up drowning everything. His head was barely above water. Della thought he resembled an elf. She was noticeably quiet after they hugged, prompting Richard to ask if she was okay.

"Yes," she said a bit hesitantly as they, Michael, and Troy poked along to baggage claim to collect Richard's wheelchair. Finally, she asked, "Do you always dress like this?"

Richard explained about the volunteer who had helped him get ready. He threw in a smile to help his cause.

Della knew he sensed her awkwardness, so she said, "Don't worry. Just keep talking—your voice is my familiar friend." It was true. For months, they'd only spoken on the phone and exchanged emails. They'd seen photos of each other online, yet it was his voice, slurred speech and all, she knew best. She'd fallen for his sense of humor, kindness, and compassion, not to mention his perseverance, so connecting all of those staggering traits with his mangled, elfish body took a minute. But she was in good hands. Richard would gladly talk her ear off if that was what it took to win her over.

At first, Michael was shy around Della, and when they got to her house and met her three daughters and son, he didn't say much. Eventually, though, he peeked out of his shell. Before long, they couldn't shut him up. Like father, like son. Everyone was impressed with how bright and helpful he was.

While Michael was adjusting to his new scenery, Troy was more than willing to pick up the socializing slack. He wanted to lick every leg, hand, and arm like they were coated in peanut butter, and to show the crowd all the neat tricks in his repertoire. However, for every lick, Richard yelled "Aaah!" which sounded a lot like the interview with the reporter. I was glad I missed a repeat performance. Troy was simply excited to meet new people and needed to be reminded he was on duty. This wasn't a vacation—he had a job to do.

After lunch, they all drove to the Gaylord Opryland Hotel in Nashville about an hour away to do a little sightseeing. While strolling around, the excitement, anxiousness, intensity, and lack of sleep of the day, on top of a full tummy, hit Richard like a haymaker and he was out cold. All engines immediately shut down. He fell asleep in the hotel's botanical gardens, while the rest of their group milled about waiting for him to wake up.

When he finally came to, they ventured over to Opry Mills mall, where Richard accidentally peed on the floor by a kiosk. It wasn't his fault; Michael had emptied his urine bag but forgotten to seal the bottom after strapping the pouch back on his ankle. The next time Richard relieved himself, urine ran straight down his leg onto the floor. Employees of the mall blamed the accident on Troy, who wasn't offended in the slightest by the unjust accusation. Instead, he tried to lick their hands as they pointed at him.

Richard, Michael, and Troy stayed at a hotel in Manchester, but unfortunately, Richard's lack of an attendant made it extremely difficult on Della. Michael could do only so much, and besides, it wasn't right to ask a ten-year-old to bathe his dad or help him use the bathroom. Since none of Richard's attendants could make the trip, Della drew the short straw. She and her son, Daniel, had to give Richard a bath and put him to bed each night. However, it wasn't until later that Richard finally got a portable lift, so Della and her son and a few gracious volunteers had to hoist Richard all by themselves. One night, Richard ended up on the floor during transition but was unharmed. Another day, Richard got his chair stuck on the ramp of the van he'd rented for the visit, and they had to ask strangers to rescue him.

None of this fazed Richard because emergencies were a regular part of his life. This was normal. It would've been unusual if nothing had gone wrong. But Della wasn't used to this. She'd been looking forward to spending Thanksgiving with her new boyfriend, not bathing him. It was a lot for her to handle. I felt incredibly guilty that I couldn't be there to help, and I was more worried than ever about Richard's proposal. It definitely didn't seem like the right weekend to pop the question.

But Richard was in gear and there was no stopping his racecar.

Over the next two days, they visited an aquarium in nearby Murfreesboro, had their big Thanksgiving meal with Della's family, and spent a lot of time getting to know each other better.

Then it was time for phase two of Richard's Master Plan.

Unbeknownst to Della, Richard had bought tickets for the two of them for a dinner cruise on the General Jackson Showboat in Nashville. It was one of the largest historically recreated paddle-wheel boats in the country. The cruise lasted four hours down Cumberland River, with authentic southern cuisine and live acts, and Richard had arranged for the manager of the restaurant to play a role in his plan.

Richard wasn't the greatest at keeping secrets. He was like a little kid who'd crammed a bunch of candy in his mouth. Halfway to Nashville, his grinning and giggling were too much for both Della and him to stand, so he confessed their destination. Della was elated to learn they were dining on a cruise, which made Richard ecstatic. All was proceeding fairly smoothly with phase two.

However, when they got on the boat, they were seated for dinner behind a pole with an obstructed view of the act, which did *not* please Richard. This was simply unacceptable. Did they understand what was happening here tonight? Phase two was in motion! Hadn't they been briefed on the Master Plan? Heads would roll.

Richard sprang into action. He and Troy weaved their way through the tables, as Della looked out at the river enjoying the view. The next thing she knew, four waiters were collecting their place settings and drinks and moving them to a table beside the stage. She saw Richard with the manager in the back of the room overseeing the operation. Troy was all business, too—no licking.

Their meal was lovely, and as far as Richard could tell, Della didn't suspect a thing. Though, he knew she was smart and it wouldn't have shocked him if she'd pieced it together. In reality, Della had her suspicions he was going to propose, but she wasn't certain. To her, it seemed like the perfect setting for such a grand moment, yet it was still early in their relationship and he might have wanted to wait until the following year.

Richard wait? Really? Until next year?! That was definitely not happening.

After dessert, it was time for phase three of the Master Plan. This was the terrifying part, more for me than for Richard. Even though I was back in Fort Worth, I knew what time the boat left, when they were going to eat, and when he was going to propose. I'd helped him set up the cruise. So I was nervously watching the clock while praying I didn't see anything on the national news that night about a man in a wheelchair zooming off the General Jackson Showboat into Cumberland River.

Richard signaled the manager, who brought a stuffed panda bear with an engagement ring tied to him. She placed the bear with the ring on the table in front of Della. Richard could hardly contain himself. He was bursting at the seams, smiling, laughing, shaking, drooling, and clapping all at once. Before Della could even reach for the bear, he blurted out a proposal.

Now came the hard part, the fourth and final phase: her response.

I was practically on my knees in my bedroom cheering them on like I was watching the whole event live on *The Truman Show* with the rest of the world. Of course, I later learned that hardly anyone dining nearby Richard and Della even noticed what was happening. They were all simply enjoying their meals and the wonderful view and had no idea that the man in the wheelchair was about to have his dream come true.

Della said yes.

Mission accomplished! The Master Plan was a success. I would've jumped up and down had I known the moment it happened, but when they called and told me, I did a few fist pumps to celebrate. I congratulated them, and told Della I couldn't wait to meet her in person. Richard yelled into the phone, "See, I told you it'd work! You gotta trust me." Then he started laughing and coughing for twenty seconds.

After their meal, the scheduled act began, which must've felt a little anticlimactic after what had just transpired, but Richard and Della still enjoyed it. It was a Christmas show, complete with traditional, Christian, and contemporary songs. Richard especially loved the Christian numbers, singing along loudly. He was having the night of his life. Troy must've felt the weight of the world slide off his shoulders now that everything had worked out according to plan because he lay down to listen to the music and drifted off to sleep. The noise and chatter and music all around him didn't bother him one bit. He could snooze anywhere.

Like father, like son.

My new band with Bryan and Manya out in Dallas was a work in progress. For the first five months, we were exclusively a garage band. Literally. We never played anywhere but in the garage of Manya's house. We just practiced. A lot. It was fine with all three of us for different reasons. I wanted to work up two sets of material before we started playing gigs because I knew once we began performing, we wouldn't have as much time or interest in rehearsing. I also thought it was essential we learned the songs cold because we'd be nervous when we started playing live and if shows didn't go well, we might lose momentum. Bryan was swamped with schoolwork and barely keeping all of his plates spinning between classes, his new part-time job at the seminary's physical plant, and working on parts for our songs.

Manya possessed one of the best voices I'd ever heard, not just on tape but in person, too. There was no drop-off in the quality of her voice, and she very rarely missed a note. She was amazing. I thought we'd lucked out and found a professional singer who just happened to be a stay-at-home mom. She took care of her daughter during the day and practiced with us two or three nights a week. I couldn't figure out why she was willing to play with us. Why was she not a solo star already? She had everything necessary to make it as a singer: a consistent voice, unique tone, range, and command, plus she was attractive with an outgoing personality. One night while driving home from practice, I told Bryan, "She could get a following in about a month. Nothing's stopping her."

Except one thing: confidence.

She hadn't played very much in front of people, and she needed to build her fearlessness, which was another good reason for us to rehearse a little extra before hitting clubs. So each Tuesday and Thursday evening and Saturday morning, Bryan and I loaded our old Ford Taurus station wagon with my keyboard and stand, our amps, guitars, cords, and the rest of the equipment we'd accumulated through the years.

We'd started buying the gear back in Atlanta for our first band, Sticks of Stonewall. I'd thought of the name Sticks and Stones, but it was taken, so this was the next best thing. I should've thought longer because none of us really liked it. That was mistake number one. Mistake number two was my refusal to play any cover songs. I only wanted to do original material and not be a human jukebox. I was pretty naïve and close-minded and didn't understand that mixing in a few songs people actually knew and enjoyed was a *good* thing and would only make them more receptive to our songs.

Mistake number three was my unreceptiveness to the other guys in the band writing songs. I didn't try to forbid anyone from pursuing it, but I certainly didn't encourage it. Since Bryan was a really good guitarist and Winn and Tripp were good vocalists, I felt the best thing I had to offer was my songwriting. If I wasn't doing that, what was I providing? Again, this was shortsighted, narrow-minded, insecure thinking that did way more harm than good. Instead of the rest of the band feeling invested because they had songs of their own in our catalogue, I alienated and frustrated them, especially Winn. Over time, everyone's enthusiasm for the band waned, and this was one of the reasons. Any venture could still be fulfilling and fun without success, but not without ownership.

As if these blunders hadn't done enough damage, I dumped a few more logs onto the fire. I wouldn't write love songs, or anything resembling a sappy ballad. I called them GAG songs

(Guys And Girls) and instead churned out one angry, depressing song after another. Bryan helped in this department. His despair and gloomy outlook on life led to many requests for songs about child abuse, suicide, or rape—all reliable crowd pleasers. We had a set list full of pain. We were perfect for funerals and breakdowns.

On top of that, my dirges were slow and long, providing the perfect opportunity for listeners to nap. It was as if I was challenging an audience, daring them to like our songs. *Go ahead, you think you're tough—try digging these songs. Good luck.* I made one blunder on top of another until four years later the band was done. For many years afterward, I lugged around guilt over my mistakes and felt I'd poisoned our dream. I wanted another chance to do it right, to learn from my bad judgment.

The band in Dallas was my second chance, just as Richard and Della had gotten theirs. I was determined to do the opposite of everything I'd loused up in Atlanta (again, the George Costanza approach). This time, I let our singer pick the band name, Blue Petal, and she and Bryan could write as many songs as they wanted. The more the merrier. If someone wanted to play a cover song, sign me up (though nobody really did). I wrote more up-tempo, positive songs. I encouraged everyone to keep working on material and to practice, practice, practice. I did whatever I could to help prepare us for the shows ahead, because I understood we operated in a sliver of space that would soon vanish and probably not come again, at least for Bryan and me. We were older now, and it had taken nine years for the chance to resurface.

We used to think it was easy to re-form, to start again, yet too many unpredictable, uncontrollable factors needed to align for it to be possible. Life had a way of persistently luring or lulling, with few pauses to redirect. This felt like our last chance to move closer to the goal we'd first set long ago in school, when there was an abundance of time and promise. Back when our hair was longer and we imagined music videos for our songs and elaborate covers for our albums and endorsement deals with guitar companies and benefit concerts for noble causes and all the crowds sang along because they knew every word by heart.

CHAPTER SEVEN

Down from the Ledge

In January, Della and her two youngest daughters, Evelyn and Emilee, moved to Fort Worth. It would've been hard for Richard to leave town because his CLASS program was simply too valuable and rare to give up, and he'd been on a waiting list to get accepted. If he moved, they wouldn't hold a spot for him if he wanted to return. He'd head to the back of the line for at least a year's wait. Plus, he wouldn't get the same amount of benefits next time, as his "cap" would be lower. Most other states didn't offer nearly as many attendant hours and services for the physically challenged as Texas, so leaving would've made life much more difficult for Richard and, consequently, everyone.

Della and her daughters rented an apartment just across the railroad tracks from Richard, and the girls settled into their new schools. I liked Della right away. She was a natural optimist, with one of the most positive, mild-mannered personalities I'd come across. She had a wonderful sense of humor and seemed to be able to laugh off the stress of leaving behind her two oldest kids, who were living with their dad, to move to a strange, new state to be with her fiancé with cerebral palsy. Inside, she was a little more worried than she let on, which was understandable, yet she kept it to herself to be strong for her girls and for Richard. If I'd been in her place, I would've been yanking my hair out that I'd possibly just made the biggest mistake of my life. Second-guessing would've been my morning ritual.

But not Della. She'd been through a lot in her first marriage and had learned to survive on her own without the albatross of regret. She understood that no one lived a perfect life free of missteps and consequences and that the more time she spent dwelling on what was lost, the more slipped through her fingers. Relocating to Texas to marry Richard certainly wasn't the safest move, but it was what she felt was right, and that was enough to justify any future problems.

I actually thought she was the perfect match for Richard. Her easygoing, calm demeanor balanced his intensity and impatience. Her relaxed approach slowed his gallop. She made him laugh, and he felt honored that she was willing to leave her home, and her kids, just for him. She softened his edges. He smiled even more with her around. He looked like a rolling jack-o'-lantern.

She also helped ground him when he was set to launch into orbit. This was never truer than when he took Evelyn to get some affordable dental work done over at La Gran Plaza de Fort Worth. It was the Hispanic mall in town and reminded me of when Bryan and I had lived near the border of Mexico. Out of curiosity, we'd once ventured across to Matamoros for half a day so Bryan could try to find a cheaper supply of Zoloft. Too bad he'd never managed to connect with the Mafia—they could've hooked him up.

La Gran Plaza de Fort Worth was quite similar to areas I'd seen south of the border. If New York had Little Italy and San Francisco had Chinatown, this was our Little Mexico. It used to be called Town Center Mall, but in 2004 new ownership took over and transformed its image. The exterior was remodeled to look like a Mexican village. Dillard's gave way to El Mercado. Fiesta Mart replaced Winn-Dixie. Most of the mall's interior resembled a bazaar/flea market. Mariachi music blared on the overhead speakers. It was busy and loud and warm, with pungent aromas from the food court detectable in the parking lot.

Better deals could often be found at La Gran Plaza, so since money was tight and Evelyn needed a root canal, we headed over to Little Mexico. After the initial visit and exam, Richard sat in the lobby trying to sort out the details with the receptionist, Marta (as her name tag read), for the next appointment. She struggled to understand what he was saying, so naturally, she wanted to talk to me. I explained that I could help clarify a word here and there, but I couldn't speak for Richard and that she needed to talk to him. He was in charge. I'd learned my lesson.

I thought.

After fifteen minutes of getting absolutely nowhere and with a line forming behind us, all parties involved grew extremely restless and agitated. Richard's speech slurred worse and became trickier to decipher when he was upset, which of course, made it harder for Marta to comprehend. She enlisted the aid of a coworker, who couldn't shed much light on the situation. Her coworker actually seemed more interested in the Big Gulp to which she was glued. Richard was attempting to find out if they had an opening next Thursday for Evelyn, and if so, what was the latest they could start on the procedure. He whispered to me, "So we can do school in the morning." I was stunned by his dedication and wanted to applaud right there in the lobby.

All the employees were Hispanic (at least the ones I'd seen) with Mexican accents, which made it even more difficult for two reasons. First, Richard couldn't understand a lot of what Marta was saying. Second, it was hard enough to decode Richard's articulation for native speakers of English, so for anyone tackling English as a second language, Richard proved a formidable challenge. Basically, Richard and Marta talked for fifteen minutes with neither one understanding the other.

Marta thought he wanted two appointments for next Tuesday (presumably the other for himself), and a follow-up as early as possible the next morning. I wasn't sure how she'd reached that conclusion, but we were slamming into the same brick wall, giving us all a headache. Evelyn was quietly hiding in the corner, wisely pretending she didn't know us. I felt helpless and anxious, Marta felt overwhelmed and behind schedule, Richard felt misunderstood and unappreciated, and Troy felt hungry and hot (he usually was).

Somebody had to do something before security was called.

So I stepped in. Or, more accurately, stepped over Richard.

I told Marta, "Just make the appointment for Evelyn for next Thursday at four, okay?" Marta nodded enthusiastically while smiling gratefully, punching in the information on her computer. Then she turned to the next customer in line and greeted him in Spanish.

Richard didn't say a word. He steered his wheelchair and Troy out of the office, as Evelyn and I followed. He drove slowly through the mall for almost a minute without looking at us or speaking. I knew I'd blown it. I knew this wasn't going to be good, that he was mad at me, probably furious. I'd just committed the cardinal sin *again* by speaking for Richard. Much worse, in public! I'd humiliated him and made him feel three inches tall. I was about to get spanked in Little Mexico. I just hoped I wouldn't get fired.

Finally, I had to say something because his silence was torturing me. "Hey, Richard, I didn't mean to step on your toes in there. I just wanted to help out because the line was…"

"You stepped on my head!" he snapped, before speeding over to an unoccupied corner of the mall near a back entrance. I didn't know if he was headed outside to cool off or if he'd meet us on the bus or what was happening. When he stopped at the door and spun around scowling at me, waiting, I had my answer. He was taking me behind the woodshed. I felt like I did when my parents used to order me to my room to "receive my punishment" after screwing up. Dad spanked me, and my brothers, with a sawed-off golf club for particularly heinous crimes, and it looked like Richard was brandishing a 7-iron.

I told Evelyn, "You should probably wait here for a minute."

Or five.

I plodded over to Richard, reluctant to be scolded in front of everyone for trying to help. I knew I'd not followed the handbook, yet people were waiting in line. Marta had tried everything she knew. We were holding up an entire business. Cavities needed to be filled, chompers yanked, new toothbrushes passed out. Richard was single-handedly thwarting Little Mexico's dental hygiene. I'd jumped in to save the day—to save smiles! I was a hero, not a villain. I should've received a key to the mall, not a public flogging.

By the time I reached Richard, I was almost as fired up as he.

Almost.

"Am I a man?!" he hollered, his face red. We were going to be here a while. Evelyn probably should've gone for churros. That actually sounded like a nice treat after the horsewhipping. "Am I just a dummy?" Richard growled. I noticed Evelyn had sat down on a bench, clutching her bag of free goodies from the dentist.

"Of course you are—I mean, a man. Not a dummy," I answered, slightly flustered by Richard attacking with both barrels blazing. "I wasn't trying to say you weren't in charge."

"Yes, you were! Yes, you were! Yes, you were!!" he accused louder and louder in case the folks in El Mercado hadn't heard him the first time. I noticed a few shoppers glancing quizzically at us. Two teenage boys had stopped to watch the show. We should've sold tickets. Evelyn could've held an arrow spinner sign like we were on sale.

"No, I wasn't. I just wanted to get out of there." I wasn't ready to beg for forgiveness, yet I could see the veins in Richard's forehead bulged bigger the louder I defended myself. I started fearing he was going to have a heart attack.

"I decide when we go!" Richard exploded. "I'm the boss! I'm the boss!"

I needed to diffuse this bomb before Richard died or I got fired or somebody sprayed us with a fire extinguisher. I swallowed my pride, changed tactics, and said, much more meekly, "Look, I'm sorry, Richard. I know you're the boss. I'm sorry if I took over in there."

But it was too late for apologies. I learned a valuable lesson that afternoon about heated arguments: They were nuclear war in a relationship and had to be avoided at all costs because no one won them. There could be disagreements, but they shouldn't escalate into screaming vitriol that couldn't be taken back. Both sides lost far more than if they'd merely taken the high road. Whoever shouted loudest and longest gained no meaningful vindication. Nothing was proven other than shortsightedness. And the window for humility closed excruciatingly fast. It never rang as true or significant later in a fight when things had already spiraled out of control. The time for constraint and sacrifice was offered only once at the beginning when it burned the worst and, therefore, meant the most.

Richard barked, "You're not sorry. You did this before. It's too late."

That was when I thought I was fired. Richard had a history of firing attendants for one reason or another, and during my years to come with him, he axed at least ten more employees for tardiness or absences, unwillingness to do it his way, "dominating him" (as he called it, and I'd just done), poor attitude, carelessness, or some other reason. He kept folks on a short leash, undoubtedly because he didn't want anyone getting the idea they were in control. It was a reaction to being handled and run over his whole life by his parents or his ex-wife or the system. This was his time to be in charge, and he wasn't playing. He used to have a much shorter fuse and worse temper. He'd mellowed. I was sure glad I hadn't worked for him back in the day, because I would've been canned for sure.

I continued sprinting the high road as fast as possible to try to salvage the situation. "It's not too late, Richard. I'm sorry. I made a mistake. Let's just talk it out."

He swiveled his chair around and headed for the exit. "Where are you going?" I called, as more people stopped to watch our Shakespearean drama. An older Hispanic woman was talking to Evelyn, presumably asking for the backstory. We should've printed off programs.

But they hadn't missed the best part.

"Don't leave, Richard. We need to talk this out." Then I launched my most powerful ammunition: "That's what the Bible says to do."

The reverend didn't like the Good Book used against him because he stopped dead in his tracks and roared, "Aaaargh!" I thought his heart attack was hitting. He drove his chair very quickly in three small circles like he was drilling himself into the mall's floor. He looked like he was on a tiny racetrack. I had no idea what was happening. I was truly afraid he was going to hurt himself, and I regretted letting things get to this point. He was under my care on my watch. I was supposed to look out for him. That was all that mattered.

I said as calmly as I could, "Please stop. Okay? Just tell me what you're thinking."

He pulled out of his fourth trip around the racetrack and bolted for the exit. "I can't," he shouted over his shoulder. "I'm shutting down."

"Huh?" I asked, thinking his chair was running out of juice. He had to charge the battery in his wheelchair all night so it would operate for a full day, yet he was still motoring along fine. "You're what? You need help?"

"I'm shutting down! I'm shutting down!!" he kept yelling as he banged the fat button on the wall that automatically opened the door on the right. He and Troy stormed outside and disappeared around the corner.

Shutting down? I repeated to myself. I turned around to find at least a dozen people watching the proceedings. The older Hispanic woman was sitting next to Evelyn on the bench. We were better than cable.

If it hadn't been for the fact that the daughter of his fiancée was left behind in Little Mexico, Richard might've kept going. He was in no mood to talk to me anymore, and I wasn't even sure I was still on the payroll. He might've just let me find my own way home. Maybe not. He seemed to have a soft spot for me, like I was his younger brother he was molding, which was pretty accurate. In any event, Richard reappeared at the doors and waved at us to come, so Evelyn said goodbye to the older woman and we headed out.

The next day, Richard informed me that he'd been very close to "throwing in the towel" on me, but Della had applied her magic touch and cooled him off before he did anything hasty. She'd reminded him that I'd apologized, and she encouraged him to think long-term. She told him it was easier to replace a morning or night attendant than someone trustworthy who could work with him all day long and help him reach his goal of a master's degree. She said to step back and take a breath and to recall the times he'd wished somebody had extended him a little grace. She said no one was perfect, not even him. By the time she was done with him, he was laughing and back to his jovial self. She had the touch.

The more I was around the two of them, the more I envied Richard. He'd found someone who balanced him, who made him better, happier. Someone who caught him before he slipped into a mistake, who could talk him down from the ledge. An accountability partner who made life easier and offered unconditional love and support. A best friend who wasn't going anywhere. A trusted ally.

I had to admit that sounded nice.

A month or so after Della and the girls moved to town, Troy got sick. Della noticed Troy trembling and she told Richard, who immediately took him to the veterinarian. While staying with the vet for a few days, Troy got worse. One morning, Troy's condition declined to the point that the vet told Richard he was going to have to put Troy down. This destroyed Richard, but miraculously, when the vet checked on Troy later that day, he'd drastically improved.

Troy was able to come home, yet his left side remained weak and dragging. It wasn't always obvious, though it definitely affected his stamina, prohibiting him from accompanying Richard all day. After a few weeks, the vet and Richard agreed it was best if Troy retired.

This was the worst part.

Troy still wanted to help Richard. He'd been trained to do it. It was his job, identity, and reflex reaction when Richard needed assistance. If Richard dropped his empty thermos, Troy scrambled to fetch it. Richard had to order him not to do it, which only confused and frustrated the newly retired service dog. It seemed to stress Troy more not to work. He found items around the duplex and brought them to Richard just in case it helped. It was heartbreaking to watch, and more than a few times Richard cried for Troy, which, of course, made Troy want to be there for him even more.

It was clear something had to be done. It wasn't fair to Troy to let him live with Richard if he couldn't serve him. He didn't know any other way to be around his owner. It was daily torture for Troy, and for Richard.

So Richard gave Troy away to a friend who owned a farm where his ex-service dog could spend the rest of his life relaxing and roaming and snoozing, out of sight of the man in the wheelchair for whom he'd been matched and trained. The man with the loud voice and the gentle hands who rubbed his head and neck. The man he loved to climb upon to lick his face, even when told not to. The man with the young boy and the chair that rolled, in the home where he could open the front door with his nose. The man he saw first each morning, and the one he checked on once or twice during the night. The man who was his as much as he was his owner's.

Richard had waited a year and raised $20,000 to get Troy, and now that beautiful, affectionate, clever Golden Retriever was gone. But Richard didn't care about the lost time and investment; he missed the bond he and Troy shared. That was the rare, powerful aspect Richard needed most. Picking up fallen items and opening doors were certainly helpful, yet it was the connection Richard had with Troy that hurt the most to lose. Troy understood his needs and shifting moods, recognized them right away, without one word of explanation or justification. Richard's speech impairment was no longer a hindrance, as their language was unspoken, and reception unconditional. Troy was more than Richard's service dog, more than his friend. He was an extension of Richard, a part of him. His hands and feet. That was a lot to give away.

And even harder to replace.

CHAPTER EIGHT

The Quest Continues

We were ready to rock. Sort of.

After months of writing music, tweaking parts, redoing lyrics, and rehearsing until we were sick of playing the same songs over and over, we booked our first gig. It was at a restaurant/coffee house in Dallas on a Thursday night, and it felt like we were playing Madison Square Garden. Much thought went into our outfits, the set list, speaking responsibilities between songs, possible encores if the masses demanded it, and alternate up-tempo and slow numbers we could sub in should the mood call for it. We tried to leave nothing to chance. There was always the possibility that a weary record label executive could be sitting quietly in the corner eating white pizza lasagna completely unaware that he was about to hear the band he'd scoured the country for but never discovered. A unique group with an original sound he could champion to the cynical critics, steering them past the leeches and hustlers lurking to steal their ticket to glory, all the way to astronomical commercial success without losing a shred of indie underground credibility.

I actually did say somebody might be there who could sign us.

It happened sometimes.

Occasionally.

We were opening for another band, which was always harder than headlining. We had to arrive extra early, set up all our gear, do the sound check, and then push our equipment to the very back of the stage so the headlining act could set up their instruments to check sound levels. This occurred a lot in Atlanta with our first band. Sometimes we had to haul our gear off the stage and then set it back up after the big-timers were done perfecting their sound quality. The headlining act frequently got a better mix (how it sounded in the room to the audience), plus better levels in their monitors (how it sounded to the band on stage), than the opening act because they didn't want the unknown band to steal their thunder. It was a slippery slope: The first band couldn't sound awful and drive people away, yet it couldn't sound incredible and eclipse the main event. The best the opening act could hope for was to win over one or two new fans, sell a few copies of their demo, and gain some valuable experience playing live. Their time would come to get the royal treatment, hopefully.

Not to mention, the venue was typically half full for the opening act, or in our case that Thursday evening, a tenth full. The majority of the crowd was waiters and waitresses. Again, this was nothing new for Bryan and me. We'd played more shows in Atlanta for servers than fans. At first, it had been somewhat demoralizing, but then we realized the waitstaff were potential fans we needed to win over, and it actually led to a few repeat shows from their requests to management. One particularly empty show, a waiter had encouraged us to try new songs and experiment to see what worked, and several waitresses told us to play as long as we wanted because it made their shifts more enjoyable. Many of them were just like us with plans and dreams they needed someone, anyone, to take seriously. They wanted us to do well because it validated their own choices and renewed their sense of purpose. In many ways, they were our biggest fans.

So when we took the stage in the Dallas restaurant to play for a few diners and many more servers, we didn't let it faze us. They were all getting treated to the musical ride of their lives! We ripped into our opening number, playing nearly twice as fast as intended. We couldn't slow down because we were so nervous and excited and self-conscious. We were like kids racing down a hill. When we hit the last note, we should've leaned forward like we crossed the finish line.

The next song, Bryan froze and forgot his part, so he pretended like he was having trouble hearing himself in his monitor. I kept glancing over at him from behind my keyboard, wondering why he wasn't playing guitar, but all he did was point to his ear like that explained everything. His hope was that the audience would understand and sympathize. *Oh, that poor fella must be having technical issues—that's why he hit those wrong notes and stopped playing.* He fiddled with his guitar cord for two and a half minutes.

Two songs later, Manya clamped her capo on the wrong fret of her acoustic guitar, so the notes I was playing didn't fit because we were in different keys. I kept leaning down placing my ear next to my keyboard to hear the notes better, even though the sound was pumping through the monitor six feet in front of me. I couldn't figure out what was wrong. I panicked and took a page out of Bryan's playbook, tinkering with my keyboard cable like I was having connection difficulties to explain why I'd stopped playing. *Who's the sound guy here?! Fire him immediately!* It wasn't until Manya was almost finished the song that I noticed her capo was one fret too high.

The next song was a fast number I'd written on acoustic guitar, with several changes in tempo and style. It was the type of song that revolved around one instrument, and I had to play the part well. It was an ambitious undertaking, but I was pumped for the challenge.

A little too pumped. I strummed so hard and fast, the pick flew out of my fingers and nailed Bryan's leg. Thankfully, I was standing in front of Bryan's mic stand that had a pick holder he'd attached with extra picks in case of emergency (plus, he thought it was cool when guitarists flicked their extra picks into the crowd at the end of songs—we would *not* be doing that in a nearly empty restaurant).

Later, I asked a friend, who'd been gracious enough to attend, how my showcase song sounded. He said, "Uh…it was intense. You know. Real loud."

"Loud?" I asked, hoping it had made a deeper impact than that.

"Yeah, like a whole bunch of sound. Really loud sound. Like a wall of sound. With distortion."

Not so deep of an impact.

We played the whole set so fast, we finished ten minutes before we were supposed to conclude. The headliner, a regular who'd been playing there two nights a week for six months, was still finishing his dessert. With no more material to present, we momentarily looked at each other like it might be a neat trick to improvise a jam song for ten more minutes for the dinner crowd. Saner heads prevailed. Manya thanked everyone for listening, and we packed up as fast as we could.

To me, there was always something embarrassing about breaking down our equipment after a set. The audience wasn't interested in seeing it and in fact hadn't come for us at all. We were simply in the way holding up their favorite musicians from taking the stage. Plus, there was no magic, style, or hipness in winding cords and unplugging amps. It was grunt work that reminded everyone, most of all us, that we weren't U2 and there was a station wagon out back where all this gear was headed. We were sweaty, tired, and extremely self-conscious (at least I was). I wished there was a curtain we could've hidden behind to do it, but there never was. We were center stage for all to see, with no more songs to play.

The manager of the restaurant turned on some music over the loudspeakers, which helped distract the patrons as we scrambled to finish. After bagging, tying, and wrapping everything, Bryan and I began hauling equipment to our car while Manya chatted with a few of her friends who'd come to support us. I told Bryan to go mingle as well, which he was eager to do. He immediately tried to sign up a young couple to our mailing list. At one point, he pulled out his wallet and I thought he was going to offer them cash to let us email them updates.

I was glad Bryan and Manya were better at networking than I, and it didn't bother me in the slightest to lug equipment by myself to our car. I was out of the spotlight in a dark parking lot, exactly where I preferred. Besides, it wasn't like there was a drum kit and bass rig to drag out. We were only a three-piece band, for the moment, so the load was bearable.

As I wedged a bag of cords beside Bryan's acoustic guitar case in the back of our dying car, the irony wasn't lost on me. I was in a band, my second, driving back and forth to Dallas three or four times a week on little sleep with the goal of securing a record deal so we could play music for a living in front of thousands of people, yet I raced for the exit sign as soon as permitted. Why was I putting myself through this? What was the point? "Because I like to write," I mumbled (I frequently talked to myself, just not loud enough for others to notice, I hoped). It had also been my dream to be on a real tour staying in nice downtown hotels around the world, and late at night after a show when everyone was asleep, I'd sit by the indoor pool thinking. I wasn't sure what would be so important I had to think about it at three o'clock in the morning by a hotel pool, but that was a later worry. At least I'd be there, successful, with people enjoying the work I'd helped create, and not in my bedroom dreaming of the day when my choices were validated.

The socializing and hobnobbing necessary to get poolside came with the territory, which I understood. It was a package deal. I couldn't expect to win folks over hiding in the parking lot. Yet that was where I took cover, the car loaded, waiting behind the wheel for Bryan and Manya like I was the getaway driver. As I sat there checking my watch wondering if McDonald's was still open so I could get a fish sandwich and a small chocolate shake (my gig treat), I couldn't figure out if this was merely a normal aspect of my peculiar personality or something seriously off that needed major adjustment before progress could be made. And, of course, far beneath lurked the giant, menacing question I tiptoed passed to avoid waking it: Was this progress limited to our band, or was I blockading all roads to growth out of fear it might actually happen, leaving me without an alibi of my own?

Over the next few months, Richard and Della got married. Twice. The first time was in March at the local courthouse because Richard's contract was up with Section 8 housing and Della needed to marry him and move in right away to be included on his new contract. The only two in attendance for the first ceremony (besides Richard, Della, and the judge) were Troy and I, so I felt honored to be a witness. Evelyn and Emilee were in school, and Richard and Della didn't want to make a big fuss over a simple courthouse wedding. It was a matter-of-fact ceremony, more like a sentencing, where the judge appeared, rattled off a few words to Richard and Della regarding the power vested in him, and they were married. If I'd blinked more than twice, I would've missed it.

In the days following the wedding, Della and the girls piled most of their things in a storage unit and moved in with Richard and Michael. It was definitely cozy in Richard's two-bedroom duplex. For the most part, everyone got along, though Michael had a few run-ins with his new big sisters, but nothing unusual for siblings. I actually wondered how Michael was handling all of this. It had just been Richard and him for a while now. Was he jealous of the attention all three girls received from his dad? Did he resent Richard for seeking additional companionship? Was he relieved to have someone else to talk to besides Richard, someone who could chat with his dad while he played video games? I really had no idea. Michael seemed to be adjusting well to the new family dynamic and living situation, but he was a pretty upbeat kid. If he was hurt by recent events, he didn't show it. Once, while helping him with his homework, I asked how he liked his new sisters, and he replied, "They're okay. I just wish we had another bathroom."

I could understand that.

Richard was in seventh heaven surrounded by his son, new wife, and stepdaughters. Some mornings I walked in to find him camped in front of his computer with his arms raised listening to praise music like it was a Billy Graham revival. Tears poured down his face as he thanked God for all the blessings he'd received. He was the happiest I'd seen him.

Yet the joy train was just pulling out. Next stop: church wedding.

For this ceremony, everyone was invited to the small Baptist church they'd reserved a few blocks from Richard's duplex. Fancy dresses and suits were worn, a delicious reception prepared, the works. Richard even went to have his wheelchair worked on that morning so it was running perfectly for the festivities. Unfortunately, it took much longer than expected and he arrived an hour late for the ceremony. While the crowd waited anxiously, I gave Richard and Della a bonus wedding gift.

They'd asked me to play piano for twenty minutes before the ceremony, so when Richard was a no-show, I dipped deep into my catalogue and pulled out every song I knew to keep the audience from deserting. At one point, I played jazz versions of Christmas songs. Then I went back to the start of the rotation to cycle through all the tunes again. I should've set out a tip jar.

When Richard finally arrived, much to the relief of Della, it was time for the main event. Troy was brought out of retirement for one last service as he performed the ring bearer's duties. He walked down the aisle carrying Della's ring on a pillow with a ribbon he clutched in his teeth. It was quite the swan song.

Then I had to tickle the ivories again. Della had asked me to play "You Are So Beautiful," by Billy Preston and Bruce Fisher (Joe Cocker later made it famous), when she walked in, so I'd practiced diligently to learn the song in time. It was now my moment to shine, forgetting, of course, it was actually Della's moment. I eased into the intro that I'd added (as if the song needed my help), gradually building intensity throughout the first verse until I hit the chorus. Then I let her rip. I pounded those keys to squeeze out every ounce of drama, emotion, and power from the refrain so that all in attendance would feel the depth of Della's love. I almost belted out, "You're everything I hope for, you're everything I need, you are so beautiful to me." I wanted Della's family and friends to understand she knew exactly what she was doing and what she wanted and to whom she was walking down the aisle because she had…

Wait a minute! I peered over the top of the baby grand piano a few measures from finishing to discover Della was already standing next to Richard. In fact, the entire bridal party was standing there watching me, waiting for me to stop playing. I'd gotten so lost in my performance, I hadn't even noticed that Della made it to the altar in under thirty seconds and had been enjoying the show with Richard for nearly twice that long. I hadn't counted on her making it there that fast. What did she do, sprint? Was this the NFL scouting combine? Was she afraid Richard would go get more work done on his chair?

Of course, I hadn't taken into account the distance from the back of the small church to the altar wasn't that far. This wasn't Westminster Abbey. Perhaps I'd imagined Della walking in slow motion during her processional as I'd timed the event in my head. My mental music videos tended to lean toward the dramatic, with lots of slow-mo and wind. This was more likely the cause. In any event, Della had arrived safely at the altar requiring no further accompaniment, so I wrapped up the song and crept away. To distract myself from my embarrassing blunder, I took solace in the fact that at least I didn't have to break down my equipment in front of everyone. That didn't help much, though.

As I listened to the minister read from the book of Ecclesiastes, it felt surreal sitting in a church watching Richard get married. It hadn't been that long ago he was sobbing in his living room about spending the rest of his life alone. Now he'd found love and was getting hitched to someone who genuinely seemed to care about him and wouldn't hurt him. The online dating idea had actually worked. I'd just been trying to keep him from going over the edge. I was amazed. *God bless the Internet,* I thought, nodding triumphantly.

I'd been with Richard for a year now and we'd already checked off one of our three major goals: marriage. We only had to finish his master's degree and find him a job to complete the quest. There was still a lot of heavy lifting ahead of us, but if we could find him a new family, anything was doable.

I was surprised at how good it felt to spend my days helping someone make progress, putting his life and concerns ahead of mine. I'd known for a long time, since my years in Children's Church as a kid, that the Good Samaritan route was the best way to go. But actually doing it was a much taller order than merely agreeing with it. On paper, it looked counterproductive not to focus on my needs, yet perhaps taking my eyes off myself to notice what surrounded me was a lot more helpful. I could actually see where I was headed and what I was missing along the way. And maybe who.

The minister read Ecclesiastes 4:9-10: "Two are better than one…if either of them falls down, one can help the other up. But pity anyone who falls and has no one to help them up." Maybe it was the verse or being at a wedding or seeing Richard and Della so happy together or just that I was getting older or a little of all of it, but I could feel my attitude toward marriage shifting. It no longer looked like a bear trap or a prison sentence that would steal my freedom forever. Working with Richard had shown me that what appeared to be a wrong turn was often a shortcut. Maybe that was how it went on the road less traveled—no on-ramps to the freeway, just shortcuts that had to be used to be seen. One step was all it took, like the day I met Richard, and this was starting to feel eerily similar.

CHAPTER NINE

Abandoning the Unsinkable Broken Boat

It didn't take long for two things to happen: Richard wanted another dog; and everyone wanted a bigger house. The second came much easier than the first.

Richard and Della had sixty days or less before their paperwork was finalized with Section 8 to find another house in the program with more rooms and space, or else they had to stay put on Wheaton Street for another year. It was go time. A third bedroom was essential, a garage to store their extra things highly desirable, and a third bathroom the dream of each child.

To aid their search, a friend of Richard's used some connections to buy him an incredibly low-priced used wheelchair-accessible van, Richard's first. The air conditioner barely worked half the time, though that was no different than my car. The lift and locking system were also primitive, supplying little more than a way to raise Richard. I called the van Big Blue, and we had to lash down Richard's chair with long straps to hooks bolted into the floorboards. It felt a little like we were transporting a maximum-security prisoner. All Richard needed was an orange jumpsuit. Big Blue offered no ramp or advanced locking system for his chair or even two useable cup holders, but it sure beat walking.

Richard and Della were motivated shoppers, not only because of the time constraints with Section 8 housing, but also with the walls closing in around them in their crowded duplex on Wheaton Street. It didn't take long before they located a house about ten minutes away with most of the features on their wish list. They signed the paperwork and it was a done deal. We were moving our base of operations and saying goodbye to the home where I'd met Richard and where we'd started our journey.

Just a month after their church wedding, I helped Richard, Della, and the girls load their stuff into their new used van and my station wagon for the drive up South Hulen Street to their new digs on North Coral Springs Drive. It took several trips to ferry everything from their old duplex and from their storage unit, yet nothing major was damaged in transit.

Their new house was in a slightly better neighborhood and provided a much-needed third bedroom, plus a garage for storage space. However, there wasn't a third bathroom, to the kids' dismay. The other downside was Richard wasn't across the railroad tracks from his beloved strip mall anymore.

This was a big deal.

Richard's independence was one of the most important factors contributing to his quality of life. His ability to leave his home on his own and travel to nearby stores by himself helped him feel unrestricted and physically able. He could walk to the store just like everyone else. He could leave and return whenever he wanted without depending on others. That was true freedom. Plus, he loved being around people, popping in and out of stores to say hi and to chitchat. But their new house was more removed from the hustle and bustle of commercial businesses. Some of the only nearby stores were CVS, Subway, and Jack in the Box. His old strip mall had Mardel's, a Christian bookstore he loved to frequent, a hair salon where he got his locks trimmed, a Whataburger with the best sweet tea, and a grocery store where he bought his victuals. And, of course, right by his duplex was East Gourmet Buffet with the finest chocolate mousse this side of Shanghai.

Now he had Jack in the Box.

Richard was certainly thankful for the van he'd received and for the home they'd found in which they could all be comfortable. He never took anything for granted, which was one of the qualities I admired most about him. In a way, he reminded me of a refugee from a third-world village now scraping by on minimum wage in the States. What would've been unacceptable to someone born here was the pot of gold at the end of the rainbow to him. Every little convenience was appreciated, no advantage overlooked. He'd missed out on so many things his whole life, he cherished good fortune in whatever form or size it arrived.

Yet potentially losing any of his independence was almost more than he could stomach. As we unpacked boxes and bags and began the process of settling in, Della could see he was down in the dumps, or as she put it, "being a poopy head."

Richard said, slightly defensively, "I'm sorry. But it's a long way to move from my friends."

This was a poor choice of words that Della pounced on when she said, "Uh, try moving from Tennessee."

This seemed to help ease the sting a bit for Richard, or at least frame his sacrifice in the proper perspective. Within ten minutes, he and I were setting up his computer at our new workstation in his bedroom, trying to untangle the little amplifier cords. It seemed I couldn't escape being a roadie.

Now that finding a new home was accomplished, we turned our attention to the other pressing issue: locating another service dog for Richard. It was an intimidating task considering the time, money, and training necessary to acquire a service dog specifically skilled to meet Richard's needs, yet my boss wasn't worried. He'd been through this before. Troy was his third service dog. Yarrow, another Golden Retriever, had broken in Richard until he retired after ten years. Jimbo grabbed the baton, faithfully serving Richard for another ten years before retiring, followed by Troy. Now it was the next runner's turn in the relay race.

It was easy to think Richard should drop it. We were busy with school, he'd just gotten married, Michael probably needed extra attention during the blending of families, Evelyn and Emilee had to get to know their stepdad, and there was a whole new neighborhood to learn and a church home to find. Not to mention the other odds and ends of transitioning into a different house. There was plenty on Richard's plate to keep him busy. Besides, how much did Troy actually do? Most of the time he napped next to Richard. With three kids, three attendants, and a wife around, didn't Richard have enough help? Was it really imperative he immediately find another service dog? Wasn't it selfish and greedy to ask for more donations? Was he thinking only of himself?

From the outside looking in, this was a natural reaction to his situation. Even from the inside, I found myself wondering these same things. I felt guilty, like I was betraying Richard, yet I couldn't stop the traitorous thoughts from crossing my mind. It seemed like more than he needed, more than enough.

But that was the whole point. From someone else's perspective, Richard should've been content and grateful to receive government assistance and generosity from friends and loving support from his family. He was a lot better off than many others with terminal illnesses or mental challenges or excruciating daily pain or the absence of any family or friends. Compared to them, Richard was doing just fine.

Yet that didn't prohibit him from wanting more like the rest of us. His physical challenges didn't disqualify him from seeking complete fulfillment. Just because he'd already received plenty of help didn't rule him ineligible for more. And his CP and wheelchair definitely didn't lower the acceptable standards of joy.

I thought of Leonard Cohen's words (one of my all-time favorite lyricists) in "Bird on a Wire": *I saw a beggar leaning on his wooden crutch. He said to me, "You must not ask for so much." And a pretty woman leaning in her darkened door, she cried to me, "Hey, why not ask for more?"*

Most people didn't ask for what they wanted. They secretly envied those who did and regretted their inhibitions or guilt or just plain cowardice that stopped them. I knew I did. How many girls had I wanted to ask out through the years but never did? Anna in the fifth grade, Karen in the eighth, Vanessa in tenth, Amy in twelfth, Janice, Danielle, Mindy, and Brenda in college and graduate school. And they were merely the ones I remembered—there were more. I was so scared of them saying no, or yes. Being rejected or breaking up weren't worth the misery. Staying alone was safer. It was enough.

My fear of change had helped push me down the road less traveled. It wasn't so much defiance of the system and a commitment to my dreams as fear of technology. I didn't like to admit this to myself, but I knew the truth. The world in which I'd grown up rebooted when I graduated from seminary to a digital planet run on computers, of which I knew little more than they connected to this new craze called the Internet and everyone now owned a laptop. Rather than sign up for a class to learn how to use one, I clung to typewriters and notepads like I owned stock in them. When everyone started carrying cellphones, I refused to buy one for nearly ten years because I was afraid to learn how to operate it. It wasn't that I didn't want to know how, didn't wish I was on the other side of the door laughing and carrying on with the rest of the party, I just couldn't bring myself to knock. With each passing day and new technological advancement, I fell a little further behind, and it felt that much more impossible to catch up.

People like Richard were courageous to me, not self-absorbed. He wasn't being greedy, he simply had the guts to ask, regardless of how it might be received or perceived. He had the will to ignore embarrassment as if it didn't apply to him and carried no votes in the outcome, which it didn't. Whatever happened was up to him and he was going to find out either way. It wasn't enough not to know. There was no such thing as enough for Richard's kind. They were the ones throwing the party.

So when it came to fundraising for a new service dog, Richard pulled out all the stops. He turned himself into a human billboard. We adorned him and his wheelchair with laminated paragraphs we'd written explaining why he was raising money. He sold T-shirts made by a friend with his favorite Bible verses. He negotiated deals with managers of local stores who allowed him to solicit donations and to sell shirts by the entrances for certain time periods every day. He camped outside these stores in his chair baking in the midday sun for hours, sucking down sweet tea from his thermos while trying to raise a few more bucks toward Troy's replacement. When my band recorded our first five-song demo late that summer, Richard asked to sell some of our CDs and to split the profits, to which I agreed. He even wore a sign that read I'M NOT DRUNK, I JUST HAVE CP as an icebreaker to win over folks. He did whatever he could to inch closer to his goal of a new service dog.

Even when we were out running errands totally unrelated to fundraising, he always wore his signs and paragraphs hoping someone might be intrigued enough to inquire. He stored extra T-shirts and CDs in his backpack strapped to his chair's handles in case he got on a roll and merchandise flew off the shelves. I took him to different shopping centers with stores he hadn't haunted so new customers could be found and old ones wouldn't run for cover. He emailed and called dozens and dozens of friends and associates about his mission to acquire a new dog.

He was determined not to settle, even if his hard work didn't pan out in the end. He would see it through. This was one of the most important lessons I learned from Richard during our years together. What could be lived with or without wasn't the correct compass for navigation. It was merely plugging holes in a leaky boat. Perseverance wasn't synonymous with progress. What mattered was the choice itself with its intended target. Where was all the toil to be channeled—survival or discovery? More was typically learned from failures and heartbreak than triumphs, but they had to be risked first. My broken boat in the middle of the sea wasn't going anywhere, yet it remained afloat. It looked and felt a lot safer than the bottomless unknown surrounding me. Yet I was stuck with a compass that pointed only around, never to, one I'd been clutching since setting sail. It was the lone way I knew to travel, though I never arrived elsewhere.

It was hard to chicken out around Richard. His fearlessness made it difficult to justify waiting till next time for anything. If he could take rejection on a daily basis, why couldn't I? If he could walk boldly in a wheelchair, why couldn't I step out on faith? If he could shove worry and embarrassment out of the way to get where he needed, couldn't and shouldn't I, too? Richard held me accountable without saying a word. Simply sitting next to him each day forced me out of my comfort zone.

And so it was that at the end of my second summer with Richard, I joined the ranks of online daters. It had worked for Richard, so maybe it would be a positive experience for me, too. Plus, I liked the idea of writing a girl first before getting the chance to blow it in person. It gave me some time to stockpile goodwill in case I disappointed her six different ways later.

I perused a few sites, but some of them had a mountain of paperwork to fill out before I became "active" (just the word gave me a knot in my stomach), while others seemed more like casual hook-up spots, which made me picture whips and penicillin. I needed something less complicated and more Christian, since faith was important to me and something I was looking for in a "match" (it was going to take me a while to get used to these terms).

Finally, I came across a Christian site that was similar to the one where Richard had found Della, yet different enough that I didn't feel like I was trying to clone their love life. That would've been weird. I filled out my biographical information, interests, hobbies, dreams, goals, and preferences, and uploaded a few photos. Bryan helped me with the technical aspects of this daring operation, though initially I told no one else, not even Richard or my mom. I didn't want to jinx the undertaking by placing too many expectations on it, and I wanted to avoid letting anyone down. Plus, I didn't need the pressure of "The Great Wife Hunt" hovering over me. That definitely wasn't going to help me enjoy the process of hurling myself into the ring. This was a top-secret mission with the highest possible security clearance. Even I didn't want to know the details.

As I quickly learned, the aim was winks and smiles. Once I was out there floundering about in the digital sea for my fellow mixers and minglers to study, I could either contact somebody or wait to receive a wink or a smile. After a few days without getting either, my leaky boat was looking awfully inviting. What the heck was I doing out here in cyberspace searching for a chance encounter with romance like I was on the Starship Enterprise probing the galaxy for new life forms? What did I really think I was going to find? A time machine transporting me back to high school so I could ask out the goddess in fourth period who didn't know my name? This was nuts. Even worse, it was a cruel new brand of torture the Digital Age delivered right to my bedroom, leaving me no escape.

I knew what I had to do. It was what Richard did when he got on his site, though it hadn't taken him a week and a half to pull the trigger—more like a minute and a half. I had to find someone promising and shoot her my best wink. Or smile. Which one? This was a whole other riddle I hadn't anticipated. Did one send a slightly different message than the other? Did a smile merely inform her I thought she seemed nice, while a wink purred a dinner invitation? What if I doubled up and used both? Did that seem desperate? Smothering? Did it violate online dating's unwritten rulebook, like waiting three days to call a girl after getting her number in the real world? My natural inclination was to use a wink, smile, wave, fireworks, and any other emoticon I could get my hands on to cover all my bases, plus an essay on my childhood and a top-ten list of my favorite road trip songs. But that was the old me, and now I was doing the opposite of what I normally would. It was smooth operator time. I even turned on Sade as I searched for the lucky lady to receive one of my smiles.

Then I turned off the music because I felt like I should have a moustache, with my shirt unbuttoned revealing a gold chain.

It wasn't as easy to find someone to contact as I thought it'd be. I figured there would be plenty of attractive girls with intriguing profiles, which there were. That was the simple part. I needed to find someone who either lived nearby or didn't mind a long-distance relationship, or the fact that I wasn't twenty-five anymore. Or that I worked as a caregiver and was an unsuccessful artist with no money living with my friend's parents, with a car on life support. Whose biggest accomplishment to date was living in South Florida, with no promising prospects on the horizon. And no health insurance.

Who wouldn't want to sign up for that?! Wow! I'd laid waste to the competition.

I was ready to delete my account and become a monk. A life of solitude, prayer, and contemplation sounded pretty good. I did enjoy the Gregorian chants my dad used to listen to while reading before bed, though it felt like one of us was about to be sacrificed. Perhaps I'd apply to a monastery, use Richard as a reference. Maybe he could sell his T-shirts out front from nine to noon. Anything was better than being reminded my life was an unappealing failure no one wanted to sample. *Dive right in, folks, there's plenty for seconds.*

What stopped me was Richard's words: "Let the girl make up her own mind." Not to mention his, and my mother's, advice not to borrow trouble. My own personal motto was *Hope for the best, expect the worst.* However, this generally locked the door before even attempting to open it. If I assumed disaster was imminent, why proceed? I needed to pry my mind ajar to the possibility that maybe something good would result from taking a chance. *Just do it,* I finally ordered myself. *It has to work because normally I'd never try this.*

After crawling through pages of profiles, I came across my moment for boldness. She stood out from the others by saying less. Her name was Leslie, she was six and a half years younger than I and lived in Memphis. She posted only one picture (beautiful), but what really grabbed me was she wrote that she wanted to find someone who'd put her second. "Second?" I asked out loud, hoping she'd hear me and explain. She did. She wrote she needed to be second after God. She wanted a guy who was so close to the Lord that everyone else, including his sweetheart, had to wait in line because there wasn't any room at the front for others.

That was different. She didn't strike me as the type who took a lot of selfies.

I was intrigued. More than that. I wanted to contact her right away before some sleazy Satanist slithered in pretending to love Jesus. Nobody loved the Big Guy more than me! *You best back off,* I warned the computer screen.

I had to act. Someone like Leslie wasn't going to stay on the market long. I could see from her profile that she'd joined the site roughly when I did, so it was only a matter of time before smoothies deluged her with winks and smiles. *Back off,* I threatened once more.

Much handwringing followed over which approach was appropriate, forward, or just plain cheesy. I ruled out a wink pretty quickly because she didn't seem like the sort of girl who'd respond favorably to it in an introduction. I strongly considered sending her only a smile and letting it breathe. Hands off the wheel, no overdoing it, let her come to me. *Play it cool, brother,* I encouraged myself, nodding confidently. Except…I wasn't cool, or a big fan of ambiguity, and a little yellow smiley face left a lot of room for interpretation. Was it really wise to bank my entire romantic future on an emoticon?

I decided I needed to write a few words to give her a sense of who I was and why I was contacting her. If I really wanted to start corresponding with her regularly, I had to take more of a shot than a smile. If she didn't respond, at least I'd know I'd gone down swinging.

Transparency and straightforwardness seemed most effective to avoid misinterpretation, so I wrote the following: *I appreciate what you said about wanting to be second after God. I agree with that.* Then I yelled for Bryan to race down the hall to my room to yank the computer away before I drowned Leslie in two pages of exposition about my spiritual journey, theological stances, and philosophies of apologetics. Once he had a firm grip, I said, "Wait. One thing."

I reached over, paused for a moment, and hit Send.

It was out of my hands now. I had to sit and wait to see what Leslie said, if she responded at all. She undoubtedly received many messages from admirers, all of them angling for the chance to woo her. I was merely the last in line. I doubted she'd see me way back here.

And she didn't. A week passed with no response. I checked the site for messages fifteen to twenty times a day. Nothing, not even from other girls surfing for potential beaus. I felt like a homeless man living under a bridge. They could smell my stench through the connection. I should've written my profile on a cardboard sign.

Then one night while eating a chocolate pudding cup and contemplating working on a cruise ship (it'd looked like they were having so much fun on *The Love Boat* when I was a kid), I got a message from Leslie. I was terrified to click on it to learn my fate. I assumed it said something like, *Sorry, I just got engaged,* or, *You really smell—take a bath.* I reminded myself that a promising fallback career in the cruise industry had recently developed should things unravel in the next few moments. With my hand shaking slightly, I clicked on Leslie's message.

It read, *It's nice to hear you say that. Have a good day.* And then she added a smiley face.

A smile! Not a mere thumbs-up like we'd just concluded business, but a smiley face. I stared at that gorgeous, bald, yellow head beaming its pearly whites at me. True, it wasn't a wink, yet we didn't want to rush things. There was no hurry. We had plenty of time for heavy stuff like winks. For now, this was plenty.

I did wonder why it had taken her a week to write me back, yet I figured she'd just been busy. I tried not to overanalyze it, though that wasn't easy for me. It wasn't until later that Leslie confessed she hadn't written me back because she'd thrown me in the trash, literally. She'd deleted my message, uninterested in corresponding with the smelly homeless man. But for some reason, she'd later gone back through her Trash folder and dug out my note for a second look. Despite her confusion over me accidentally listing my ethnicity as Asian American, she changed her mind and decided I was worth a try. I was glad she did. It would've been agonizing choosing between the monastery and a cruise ship.

CHAPTER TEN

Adventures in Knitting

That fall semester, Bryan was rejected for his practicum. His master of arts in marriage and family counseling required successful completion of practicum to graduate. Practicum lasted two years, beginning with group work with fellow counseling students and their professor during which they learned to share openly. Later, students counseled clients while wearing earpieces so their professor could advise them during sessions. Students then counseled at other centers in the area while still being monitored, before finally getting to counsel unsupervised and reporting their work to their professor. The initial group work and sessions were held at the seminary's counseling center one night a week with a variety of clients from the community who received a discounted rate because of meeting with students.

Bryan had waited on pins and needles for months to learn if he was accepted, but now that he wasn't, he had to reapply for admission into next school year's practicum. If he was rejected for that, there was a chance he could get dropped from his program or "encouraged to explore other avenues of study," as one faculty member had put it to him.

These were dark days. The world had just bucked completely off its axis and been blindsided by the meteor from *Armageddon.*

Bryan kept his bedroom door locked most nights. When I knocked to see if he wanted to order a pizza and watch a movie, his favorite pastime, he merely mumbled, "I'm going to sleep." I sweetened the pot with bonus enticements like chocolate chip cookies and bottles of Coke (he swore it tasted better in bottles) with no luck. He slept most of the day, even at his part-time job with the physical plant. His chief responsibility was to drive around in one of their work trucks replacing air filters in all of the buildings across campus, including student housing, and every so often he parked at the very back of campus to take a nap in the truck. His motivation vanished. He stopped keeping up with his studies and practicing guitar. He let it all slide.

And why not? Without practicum, he couldn't complete his degree and counsel as a professional. His dream to open a home for troubled children was lost. His reason for going back to graduate school had just been ripped away. In that one letter, his future closed.

When the letter from school regarding practicum had arrived, I'd stood in his room as he opened it ready to applaud or to console him. The letter didn't mention why he'd been turned down for a spot in practicum, merely that he needed to reapply for completion of the program. Nice of them to remind him.

But we knew why they'd done it.

Bryan was different from his classmates—from the rest of the student body. His checkered past and arrests certainly made him unique at the conservative seminary, though there were others who'd made mistakes they were now overcoming. No one was spotless, no matter how hard they prayed or how often they read scripture. It was still a fallen world choked with sinners, and Bryan was no different in that regard. His sins were simply louder.

What set him apart was his emotional instability. At the time, he'd been diagnosed as bipolar, though he later learned he actually wasn't. His depression, anxieties, and mood swings seemed to point to bipolar disorder, yet he never had manic episodes. Regardless, the seminary had never dealt with a student with his condition, which was hard to believe, but that was the prevailing sense Bryan got within his program. He was an anomaly. Worse—a loose cannon. Basically, they worried he might get into practicum and flip out during a counseling session with a client. With his condition, they weren't sure he could handle the stress and trauma he'd have to deal with on a weekly basis. They thought it might overwhelm him. They didn't know. This was unchartered territory for them, so they thought the best thing to do was to slow the process to give Bryan another year to prepare and to prove he could stay in school doing well without setbacks.

I also believed they were testing him to see how he coped with the disappointment of not being accepted into practicum, though that was merely a theory I didn't share with Bryan. Perhaps they secretly hoped he'd flame out over the rejection and quit school, sparing them the headache of wrestling with his reapplication. After two weeks with his bedroom door locked at night, I thought they might get their wish.

During the rare moments Bryan slunk into the bathroom, I tried to straighten up his bed and stack his books to curb the chaos. I thought his messy, disorganized room contributed to his disorderly life. It wasn't the sole cause, but it sure didn't help. I had a feeling he looked at his clutter and thought, *I can't even keep my room clean. I stink at everything.*

However, trying to tidy up Bryan's room in the ten minutes he was in the bathroom was like sweeping the Sahara. His mess had gone viral. Heaps of clothes, magazines, books, papers, notebooks, backpacks, pens, Coke bottles, empty bags of chips, and beaten-up shoes smothered every square inch of space. Some piles were three or four feet deep. It was like trudging through snowdrifts. The one sliver of daylight sat directly in front of his computer, though he must've parachuted over there because the dense jungle offered no paths. It would've been simpler to torch it all and start from scratch, but Bryan was a hoarder (obviously) who couldn't discard anything. His possessions were the only thing he felt he controlled. They were his and nobody could say otherwise. He couldn't sabotage them. He couldn't screw them up. It reminded me of the way Richard acted with hiring and firing employees. That was the one area where he got to be completely in charge, where no one else could step in and tell him what to do. Bryan's mountainous mess was just that: his. It wasn't pretty, yet if it helped him keep going, I was all for it. I waded out of his room and shut the door.

During the practicum fallout, Bryan didn't even want to play tennis anymore. Besides movies, computers, and rock climbing, one of the only other hobbies Bryan enjoyed was playing tennis. He'd played in high school, and his doubles partner, Todd, lived in Fort Worth. When Bryan started back at seminary, the three of us began meeting every Friday evening to play tennis and pray together.

Maybe we should've prayed before tennis.

Bryan never thought he did anything well, whether it was school, work, remembering birthdays, playing guitar, talking to girls, paying attention to details, or playing tennis. He always focused on what didn't work. So in tennis, he saw only his missed shots, not the made ones. He compared his game to Todd's—Todd was the best player of the three of us—as if he needed more ammunition with which to bombard himself. As much as he loved the game, he seemed to hate playing it even more. Yet he never wanted to give it up. I thought it afforded him the rare opportunity for quasi-validation that he, indeed, could do nothing right.

And he took full advantage of the chance.

One Friday night on a public court near Todd's house, Bryan missed several shots in a row before finally slamming his racket to the ground and sprinting to the back fence. I didn't know where he was going because there wasn't a door there and the fence was fifteen feet high. He looked like he was going to try to plow right through the fence. Yet when he reached it, he became Spider-Man and climbed eight or nine feet straight up the wire netting until he was approaching the top (he was definitely a good climber). Then he stopped and shook the fence while wailing like he demanded his freedom from the tennis court. He let go with his left arm and swung it wildly over his head while turning back to us. He looked like King Kong on top of the Empire State Building swatting at planes. The two people playing on the court next to us stood with their mouths hanging open while clutching their rackets to defend themselves against the great ape.

After a few more moments of brawling with the fence, Bryan climbed down before a crowd could gather. I waved at the other players to apologize, yet they were already packing up their bags to leave. Apparently, they'd seen enough and wanted to flee before King Kong got hungry.

One Saturday afternoon, we played on a court at a local high school and I tried to arc a lob over Bryan standing at the net, but it wasn't nearly deep enough, setting him up for an easy smash. Unfortunately, when the ball dropped to Bryan, he swung and missed it completely. Rather than try to hit the ball again before it bounced a second time, he just kept swinging in the same spot like he was wielding a pick-ax on a chain gang. When clobbering air wasn't sufficient, he stepped forward and began assaulting the net with his racket. Todd told him to knock it off, so Bryan stomped over and sat in the corner of the court against the fence.

Todd and I weren't exactly sure what to do or say. We'd seen Bryan's "losing it" episodes (as Bryan referred to them) before, and we knew he needed time to cool down. It usually took him a few days to tunnel out of Funk Town, so nothing would be resolved right away. It was tempting just to keep playing while he fussed and fumed. Yet we couldn't enjoy ourselves with him stewing.

We walked over and sat next to him, trying to think of ways to encourage him. I said, "Bryan, I've missed so many easy shots, it's pathetic. Happens to everybody."

Todd added, "We really shouldn't be playing with the sun directly over our heads. Makes it tough to hit overheads and serves."

None of this made much of a dent, as Bryan continued sulking silently. We sat beside him with our sweat pouring into our eyes and off our legs onto the scorching court. Todd peeled off his sticky shirt and wrung it out next to him. I wished we were in the shade for the intervention. I desperately tried to think of how I could help Bryan understand that he wasn't alone when it came to mistakes and poor choices, and that he had a lot to offer from his experiences. I just couldn't land on the right words.

Thankfully, Todd found them, and right in the nick of time before we drowned in our own perspiration. He said, "You know, Bryan, you're too hard on yourself. I wouldn't even be a Christian if it wasn't for you." It was true. Todd had smoked pot and was a drinker in high school until Bryan led him to Christ. Bryan hadn't given up on Todd, wouldn't leave him alone until he came around. Todd said, "I'd still be smoking weed. You don't have any, do you?"

This cracked a smile in Bryan's iron mask. Todd began retelling a story of how Bryan once chased him around their hotel on a field trip for Spanish class because Todd was wasted and Bryan wanted to keep him out of trouble. Todd mentioned how, even after becoming a Christian, he still struggled with pot and would call Bryan to come over and make him flush it down the toilet. Bryan couldn't help but laugh at these memories, and he slowly began dragging himself out of the emotional dumpster.

There were other episodes on tennis courts scattered all over Fort Worth (Bryan didn't discriminate), yet for several weeks after he was denied practicum, Bryan wouldn't touch his racket, wouldn't do much of anything. Nothing interested him except hiding. He was a hollowed-out shell who'd been granted the perfect excuse to fold. This was the genuine validation he sought that he loused up everything and was better off not trying. He was done hoping and trying for more. It only worsened the disappointment later.

I didn't know how to reach him, what to do. Neither did his parents or Todd. But one thing was certain: If he flunked his classes this semester, he was definitely done. If he could keep passing, maybe the school would come around next year and grant him admission into practicum. It was his only shot, so I took a page out of my time working with Richard and began tutoring Bryan every day after work. At first, he wouldn't let me in his room. Then he let me talk only briefly. Then I graduated to sitting down (though that was easier said than done in his room), until we finally began examining his assignment lists to identify the damage. It was bad. He had four papers due in less than two weeks, plus a test and a presentation. He muttered, "Just forget it."

Yet I told him the same thing Richard had said to me when we first started working together: "We can at least try."

So we did. We worked for several hours each night on different assignments for the next two weeks. Richard had prepared me well for late nights under tight deadlines. Bryan slowly picked up steam as he got a little more done on a paper or on his presentation. I quizzed him on terms for his test, edited drafts of his papers, reviewed his delivery and slides during many runs through his presentation, and guzzled lots of coffee. We even straightened up his room a little as we went. Just a little.

By the end of the two weeks, he'd turned in all four papers on time, taken his test and passed, and given his presentation for a solid A-. He'd survived the storm, and his dejection was now replaced with determination to be accepted into practicum next time. I didn't know how long his optimism and zeal would last or what unforeseen crisis might trip him up again, but we'd just have to grind our way through it then. One thing I'd learned from Richard, and from Bryan, was that hope didn't ride in on a white stallion to save the day. It sat over in the corner of a blistering tennis court or on a Help Wanted ad in a school lounge waiting for an opportunity to prove itself. It was a two-man operation requiring more than belief. It needed a hand getting off the ground.

It was around our second Christmas together that Richard made the weirdest request I'd ever received. I actually wasn't sure I'd heard him right and asked him to repeat it. And then again. Yet it didn't improve with age like fine wine. There was nothing fine about what he wanted from me. I shook my head, and said, "Are you serious?"

"Why not?" Richard asked with a grin. Even the man without inhibitions grasped the awkwardness and inappropriateness of what he suggested. We were way off the reservation with this.

Yet I couldn't turn him down. He wouldn't have held it against me, but I knew he didn't really have anyone else he could ask for help with this particular task. It was far different from helping him eat a salad or use the bathroom or donating toward his service dog. This was about as unusual as it got.

So I lashed him down in Big Blue and we headed to the bookstore. On the way, I prayed silently that we wouldn't be caught and thrown out. I could very easily imagine someone taking a cellphone photo of us being escorted out and posting it to the worldwide digital scrapbook with a detailed explanation. It would be hard for Richard to explain this in Sunday school, or for me to help Leslie understand. I barely made sense of it.

Richard wanted us to find the *Kama Sutra* and discover alternative sex positions he could explore with his new bride. When he'd asked me, I felt like I did when I was about to wipe his booty for the first time. Everything went white hot and clammy. However, this wasn't a kinky, freaky, weird-o-rama thing. This was a genuine need born from his unique circumstances. His increasingly large belly (married life agreed with his appetite) coupled with his cerebral palsy and inability to use his legs limited what he and Della could do sexually. So, he needed some tips, ideas, diagrams, and step-by-step instructions he couldn't find on his own. He needed my help with an intimate aspect of his marriage, which was actually an honor when I looked at it that way. Which was why we were now walking into Barnes & Noble.

He couldn't do this with Della because she'd taken a job at Chick-fil-A, plus he wanted to surprise her with his findings. He was like an explorer in exotic, untamed lands. He was taking the initiative in this highly sensitive area that probably would've been too embarrassing for Della to investigate in public. But not for Richard. He was up for anything, as I learned each and every day.

As casually as possible, we strolled through the bookstore like we were there to pick up a new dog calendar. I smiled and nodded to everyone to dispel any suspicions that we were about to look at naked women together. *Nope, not us,* I assured them with my cheery smile. *He's a reverend, and I'm a seminary graduate. No nudity for us!*

After fruitless passes through the Art & Photography, Romance, Self-Transformation, and Activity Books sections, I realized what we were looking for had to be in Living Your Best Life. It was the only section left remotely related. It also occurred to me that we couldn't simply stand there in the middle of the aisle holding the *Kama Sutra* while taking notes. I knew that was too humiliating for me and I'd chicken out. We had to be more discreet for me to get through this.

So, I improvised and grabbed a large knitting book on our way to sexual enlightenment. Instantly, a wave of relief washed over me like I'd donned an impenetrable disguise. I was safe—*we* were safe from discovery. Phew! That was close.

Of course, it didn't dawn on me that two guys intently examining a knitting book in the middle of the day was probably going to look as odd, unusual, and downright strange as if we were flipping through the *Kama Sutra*, but I was ecstatic with my choice because grandmothers knitted and the book was huge. A cat could've hidden behind it, maybe with his favorite toy.

Sure enough, we found our encyclopedia of pleasure in Living Your Best Life (I was ready to). I saw the title on the spine and looked both ways like I was about to shoplift a Snickers bar. I was surprised they didn't have the book covered in a brown paper bag like the porn magazines next to the chewing tobacco (quite the combo) behind the counter at gas stations.

Transition time was key here. I had to slip the book off the shelf and behind our knitting shield before anyone spotted us. I turned to the middle of the knitting book and set it on Richard's lap so it rested against the right arm of his chair to stay open. Then I took a deep breath, scanned both ways once more, before stabbing at the *Kama Sutra* like it was made of burning coals. I missed and knocked over the books beside it like dominoes of eroticism. I started sweating. I was afraid a diligent employee would appear to assist us. They never emerged when I needed them, especially at home improvement stores, only during the rare moments I wasn't lost. *Leave us alone,* I demanded in my head. *This is a private matter.*

I shoved the books back in place, swiped the Holy Grail, practically dove at Richard's lap with it, and then glued it behind our knitting wall while draping myself over the two books pretending to read. Nobody saw a thing, and in fact, Richard didn't either because I was blocking his view. He said, "You mind if I look?"

I leaned back to grant him visual access, careful not to expose too much of the party to any curious eyes that happened by. At first, Richard didn't say anything as he perused the positions, some of which looked like gymnastics routines. How long were people supposed to stretch before attempting these? Was this the yoga instructors' edition? And the names for these stunts were simultaneously embarrassing, intriguing, and disturbing: Concubine, Dolphin, Sprout, Cello. Was a third party involved? Some assembly required? I was exhausted just looking at them.

We spent twenty-two minutes examining the *Kama Sutra*—I timed it. During our study hall, two customers dared to live their best lives along with us. They never walked past us, yet the younger one (clearly a frat boy searching for cheap thrills with no intention of reaching his best life) inched dangerously close to us when he apparently couldn't find anything good for the boys back on campus. I guarded our book like it contained the launch codes to nuclear missiles.

Richard didn't say much during our reading. I hoped to God he didn't want to buy a digital version so Computer Lady could read it to him every day for further clarification. He was going to have to catch that show solo. Probably with the lights dimmed. I couldn't make this a habit. One team viewing of a sexual guide with my boss was about all I had in me.

He did chuckle once at a particular position that seemed to defy the laws of physics, and he grunted, "Hmm," at a few other promising moves (at least I took his reaction to mean they had potential). It was incredibly difficult to discuss what we were reading, partly because it was a fairly quiet bookstore, and also since this wasn't a typical topic we covered between morning devotion and Bible college classes. I thought if one of us started talking, the other would run for his life out of shame. As long as we didn't speak, it was almost as if we were sleepwalking soldiers on a reconnaissance mission with no culpability in the events that transpired. We were just along for the ride, and when we awoke in our beds the following morning, words like dolphin wouldn't conjure up an alternate meaning and image that made it difficult to watch *Free Willy*.

When Richard had seen enough, I paused to make sure the coast was clear before ramming the book back in its spot on the shelf like they were locking the front doors to block our escape. Then we hustled down the aisle as I held our knitting book with its cover out so all could see our preferred reading material. *Yeah, that's right—men knit. Deal with it.*

As we loaded into Big Blue, Richard remained quiet until he finally said, "Thank you."

I wasn't sure, but it almost seemed like he felt guilty for dragging me into this. I said, "No problem. I check out that section at least once a week on my own. You saved me a trip." I smiled and rubbed his left shoulder. Then as I raised him on the lift, he began laughing and said, "You better not. I'm gonna stand guard at the door." He paused for a moment, and then wondered, "Maybe I could sell shirts here."

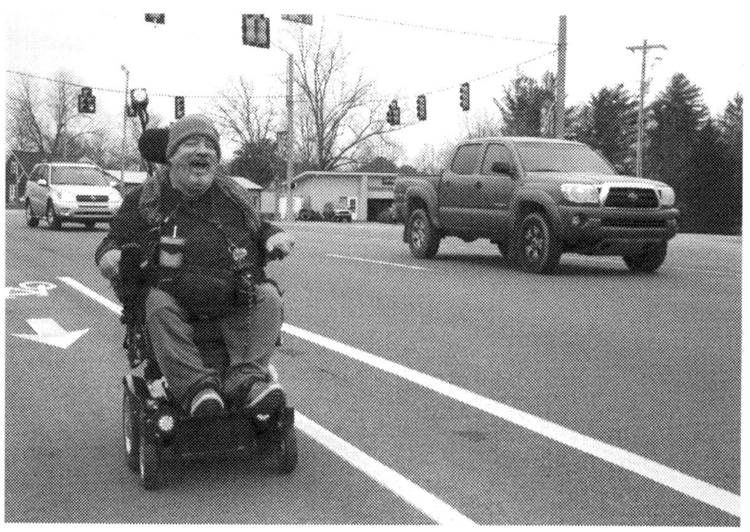

Richard, full speed ahead as always.

Richard with his bride, Della, and honored guest Troy.

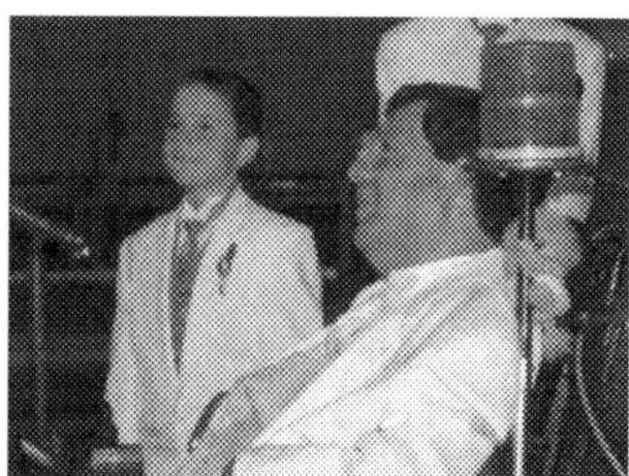

Michael standing alongside his dad at the wedding.

Me, lost in my musical moment as Della walked down the aisle.

CHAPTER ELEVEN

A Safe Haven

Our smiley faces had blossomed into paragraphs into full-length letters. Leslie and I wrote every day, except for a two-day stretch when I didn't hear from her and I was certain I'd scared her off. I had no idea how, yet her sudden disappearance convinced me I'd ruined everything. I felt like Charlie Brown in *A Charlie Brown Christmas*: "Everything I touch gets ruined." Actually, that sounded a lot like Bryan, too. I sent two extra letters to Leslie apologizing for my reprehensible remarks that had driven her into hiding, though I couldn't unearth them no matter how meticulously I combed my memory. Finally, catastrophe was averted when she let me know she'd simply been out of town for work (complicated medical stuff involving 3D mapping systems for heart procedures that I struggled mightily to understand yet hadn't a solid clue). She even called me "my worrisome friend."

We'd advanced from strangers to acquaintances to pen pals to friends.

Now we just needed to talk on the phone.

I wasn't a big phone talker. In fact, I hated it. I'd just recently bought my first cellphone, a TracFone, because Richard needed me to have one handy and this looked like the easiest to learn.

I never knew what to say on the phone, when I was allowed to exit a conversation, or how to terminate the torture. Once I said hello, I was trapped. With letters, even online chatting (which Leslie and I had just started doing), I didn't feel put on the spot as I did on the phone. I was also cozier expressing my thoughts in writing than wedging them into spoken words every few beats. The odds of me blowing it increased dramatically once I opened my mouth. However, while letters provided a sturdy, dependable foundation, I knew speaking was basically unavoidable in a relationship, though plenty of marriages had given it a shot.

Thankfully, we were progressing gradually at a cautious pace, so there was time before we played phone roulette.

At least, I thought there was time.

Leslie and I exchanged letters each day, but we scheduled one night a week for "chat" sessions. When the next one rolled around, my Internet connection was so poor we couldn't maintain a conversation without minute-long pauses during freezes. At first, Leslie suggested we try tomorrow night. Then she wrote, *Or we could talk on the phone…*

I was so caught off-guard, and so fearful of impaling myself on the phone, I typed exactly what skittered through my head: *Yikes.*

This wasn't the wisest choice of words.

Instantly, Leslie began apologizing for rushing things and making me feel awkward and reading too much into our friendship and wasting my time, and she concluded it was definitely best if we didn't contact each other anymore and she wished me the very best.

"Huh?" I grunted from the floor where her message left me. "What the heck just happened?"

I scrambled to write her back, explaining that I didn't feel pressured and I wanted to speak to her and she'd misinterpreted my *Yikes* and not to sever all ties, but the blasted Internet connection was frozen again and wouldn't melt. *I knew I couldn't trust computers,* I growled inside.

I didn't know what to do. I had no way of reaching her. We'd communicated only online. She'd never given me her phone number or mailing address or even her email address. I knew her full name, yet she'd mentioned she wasn't listed in the phone book. She was a ghost with no trail. There was the distinct possibility I'd never talk to Leslie again, and it deeply bothered me. This was the first time I realized my feelings for her had grown more serious than I'd noticed or been willing to acknowledge.

I paced around my bedroom trying to solve the riddle, each second gulping an hour. I knew the longer she didn't hear from me, her false assumptions set more firmly in concrete. I had to nip this in the bud tonight before it unraveled out of my control. But how could I reach her?

Then I saw the box she'd sent me a few weeks earlier with some thoughtful gifts, and I remembered something. While she'd slyly omitted her street address from the box, she'd scribbled down her phone number under her name. Maybe the post office had made her (drill sergeants). I hadn't even paid attention to it when the package first arrived (I was a little preoccupied with getting to my loot), but I grabbed the box and found the number. It wasn't wishful thinking—it was a postal miracle! I was so thankful a little of Bryan's hoarding had rubbed off on me and I hadn't thrown away the box. Maybe he was onto something.

I had Leslie's number—now I just had to dial it.

Normally, this would've been an agonizing, time-chewing ordeal involving many aborted attempts at pushing each imposing number, along with the green gatekeeper button, without caving in. However, I had no time for such childish games. Lives hung in the balance. I stood at full attention with my feet planted shoulder-width apart, gripping my TracFone so tightly it knew I meant business. No monkeying around this time. I had a call to make. Operator, patch me through to *mi amore*!

It rang and rang again. More ringing. Another ring. One more excruciating ring. Was this her real number? Had I been hoodwinked? I was about to hang up when her mailbox message kicked in. It was Leslie. She told me so. She said, "Hi, you've reached Leslie." Jackpot! I'd found her. I'd never heard her voice before. She spoke with a southern accent, naturally—a good Tennessee girl. But why hadn't she answered? She must've been packing for her journey out of my life, screening calls to ensure I couldn't snag her ankle on the way out the door.

When it was time to deliver my earth-shattering message, Cary Grant I was not. I fumbled and stumbled my way through a rambling apology/explanation, repeating several key points, not for emphasis, but for lack of originality. I stressed how much I enjoyed writing her, that I looked forward to it every day, and that I hoped she called me back. I wrapped up the whole shebang by giving my name, in case I'd forgotten to do so. I honestly couldn't remember.

After I hung up, I had a staring contest with my little phone waiting for Leslie to call me back. It was a long wait. Nothing happened for the next seventeen minutes. She must've listened to my message and deleted it, perhaps changed her number, or chucked her phone into the toilet like a bandit covering her tracks. Maybe she had a drawer full of cellphones and passports. Aliases from Memphis to Bangladesh. And a microchip in her left hip. Leslie probably wasn't even her real name. I was definitely losing the staring contest.

I checked the Internet connection again to see if it was still frozen and there was a message from Leslie. I couldn't believe it.

She wrote that hearing my voice on the phone had calmed her down and eased her worst fears, and that she'd never written her number on a package like that. Lucky for me, she had.

"Thank you, God," I whispered, before writing her back as fast as my fingers could type. After I sent my message, I patted the computer like it was a good doggie. The computer had found Leslie, and my cellphone had saved her. Technology and I had made up!

Leslie and I arranged to talk on the phone that Saturday evening. After our hurricane of a night, we both needed a few days to recover and reset. This gave me time to prepare for our phone conversation, which wasn't my specialty. I wrote a list of pertinent biographical data Leslie had relayed during our correspondence that I could refer to when we rapped on the phone in case I forgot anything under pressure. I didn't want to get her brother's name wrong, and I hoped to impress her by "remembering" all three of her dogs. I listed, in order, names and ages for her three siblings, three dogs, parents, aunts, uncles, cousins, and so forth, her employment and education history, church affiliation, previous dating relationships (very short list), and anything else I could recall. I typed it up in outline format with various sections underlined or highlighted for degrees of emphasis. I felt like I was either about to assassinate her or give a PowerPoint.

When the evening finally arrived to call Leslie, I locked my bedroom door, set out my list of facts, another page of questions to ask her to avoid dead air, a book of Laffy Taffy jokes (she adored them), and rehearsed my icebreaker joke I'd memorized: "What do you get if you cross a gold dog with a telephone? A golden receiver!" Bahahahahaha!!

Yet when she answered the phone, she spoke with a British accent pretending to be her sister visiting from overseas. I said,

"Ha ha. Very funny." But she continued playing the part, insisting Leslie was in the bathroom and would be right out. She apologized for the delay. She said Leslie had told her many great things about me. She wouldn't break character. The accent sounded authentic, at least compared to the James Bond movies I'd seen. I asked her how she had a British accent if she'd grown up in Memphis, yet she said she'd lived overseas for the last ten years. I scanned Leslie's dossier for anything about a sister in England but came up empty. This went on for five minutes. At one point, I even mentioned my mom had awakened me when I was little to watch Princess Diana's wedding. What was going on here?! If Leslie really was in the bathroom, what in tarnation was she doing there? Vomiting because she'd been roped into talking to me?

Finally, Leslie started laughing and gave up. She would've made a good actress. She dove headfirst into her role. I was so thrown off, I completely forgot my icebreaker joke, though it was a tad late for it now. It probably wouldn't have been that funny anyway. Good thing her sister had shown up.

By the end of our phone call thirty-four minutes later, I was exhausted, sweaty, and needed a shower. This whole talking-on-the-phone thing wore me out. How did people do it every day? I felt like I'd taken a final exam, and I wasn't even sure I'd passed. I'd tried to relax and joke around, casually dropping key facts from my list here and there, but I could've done better. I wished there was a way I could write the entire transcript for our phone conversation before we actually had it so I could merely deliver lines like an actor. That would've been much more effective. I needed to look into precognition.

But above everything else, I had to prepare for what came after the phone calls. It was inevitable and chugging 'round the mountain at breakneck speed. I had to travel to Memphis to meet Leslie in person. No lists or icebreakers or dossiers could save me then. No flash cards or Laffy Taffy books allowed. I'd be in the land of Elvis to meet her whole family without a parachute. Maybe I'd go to England to visit her sister instead.

School, school, school, school. Between Richard's relentless pursuit of his master's degree and spending my free time helping Bryan stay on track at seminary, I felt like I was back in graduate school juggling classes. My master's program in communications at seminary had included plenty of extra Bible and theology courses, so in order to graduate in two years I had to take seven or eight classes a semester. By the time I limped across the finish line, my head was spinning and I was sick of school (especially after the previous sixteen years of education—seventeen including kindergarten, which had some tricky finger-painting assignments). For several years after I graduated, I awoke from nightmares that I still had one more class to complete or I'd forgotten to turn in a paper. *Turn it in now,* I'd think for a few seconds.

The longer I listened to Computer Lady read to Richard, the more it reminded me of my endless school days. Our hours in front of Richard's computer schlepping our way through History of Christianity or Introduction to Pastoral Counseling were wearing on me. We'd been at it for a year and a half, with probably another year and a half to go. I began craving errands, even volunteering to run to the store or to the post office or anywhere Computer Lady wasn't. "You need me to go put gas in the van?" I'd ask Richard hopefully. "You don't want it running out on you and stranding you on the side of the road." Any task was fine with me.

Unfortunately, when we went out in public, we left a controlled environment for a thoroughly unpredictable one where I usually ended up in an awkward, unenviable spot that made me long for the safety of Richard's school lair.

Through a lifetime of being pushed around or ignored, Richard had learned that to be seen, he often had to thrust himself right in someone's face. So that was what he did, though not always at the appropriate time. If we were in Walmart to return something at Customer Service, he had a habit of inching his way beside the line like he was coasting by a row of cars stuck in traffic probing for the best spot to slip in. Sometimes he simply headed straight for the counter and stared at the employee handling customers until he or she asked what he needed. When we were done and alone, I tried to explain to him that it wasn't fair or polite to barge past everyone waiting patiently. His answer was surprisingly logical: "I need the manager so I can explain my situation. If I sit in line, when I get to the front, it'll take longer and everybody has to wait." I wasn't sure how to refute that, so I let it go.

Wherever we went, Richard always wanted to speak to the manager, sometimes to expedite successful clarification, other times to strike a deal. Again, Richard had learned the hard way that to survive on little income, he couldn't be afraid or too prideful to ask for help, and that if he didn't initiate, people typically didn't offer. Invariably, at some point during our conversations with managers across Fort Worth, Richard pulled out his tried-and-true sales pitch: "What can you do for me?" He reminded me of a car salesman asking a waffling customer, "What's it gonna take to put you in this car?" It was bold, direct, pushy, slightly inappropriate, and generally effective. Yet it was also incredibly embarrassing for me since I didn't possess a tenth of Richard's chutzpa.

Though as awkward as it was standing beside him during one of his negotiations, it still beat Freebirds World Burrito. Richard liked to dine here every now and then, which was fine with me because I enjoyed their food. However, Freebirds' burritos were gigantic and perfect for unholy messes if we weren't careful. I strapped on Richard's biggest bib and used both hands to feed him each bite to prevent calamitous spills. It worked pretty well, except for one time when Richard forgot to do something critical to the operation's success: bring me.

I dropped Richard off for a meeting with an old friend, while I ran a few errands for him. Then I was going to pick him up and we'd head to nearby Freebirds for lunch. However, Richard's friend was called away from their meeting and had to reschedule. Instead of letting me know he was finished early, Richard buzzed over to Freebirds alone. He was trying to make better use of time so I didn't have to stop my errands to feed him. He'd eaten plenty of meals before I was hired. He was a big boy. This was another opportunity to exercise independence.

But when he called me ten minutes into his meal because he was covered in food, independence looked highly overrated to me.

I sped to Freebirds as fast as possible and flung open the door to find disaster. It was the lunch hour, so the restaurant was packed, and seated smack dab in the middle of everyone was Richard at a small table by himself. He had on a brown leather jacket, which I'd never seen him wear before. Even more visually stunning was the absence of his bib, either the smaller one for simple meals or the "fishing net" (as I called it) for sloppy dishes. Almost Richard's entire torso was covered in burrito, not to mention his lap, wheelchair, table, and the floor beneath him. It looked like he'd been hosed down with food.

For a moment, I stood in the doorway seriously contemplating leaving. Richard hadn't spotted me yet. He probably couldn't see through the fog of food. I could've raced to Big Blue and told Richard I was stuck in traffic or the van wouldn't start or a street gang had knifed all four tires. Anything sounded better than mopping up a mess rivaling the BP oil spill.

Yet I couldn't go. This came with the territory of working with someone with CP. I had no choice but to enter the fray. I just wish he'd worn the fishing net.

The roughly eighteen feet between Richard and me was the hardest part. Once I got to him, it was just a matter of enough paper towels. Working with him in public had taught me that it was impossible to tend to his needs while worrying about what others thought. I didn't possess the multitasking capabilities to fix his problems while addressing my anxieties. He was all I could handle, which was a blessing. I probably would've become irritated and annoyed with him if I'd been able to stop and notice how embarrassed I was.

A few paper towels weren't enough for this mess. I asked the cashier for a whole roll, plus damp cloths, hand towels, rags, Wet Ones, a trash bag, sponge, and anything else she could spare before attacking Richard. I worked from his head down so all the food ended up on the floor. I washed his face until I could see it again, wiped off his neck and snazzy leather jacket, polished his hands, brushed and scooped off all the bits of burrito from his chair, scrubbed the stains on his gray dress pants with the damp cloths and Wet Ones, swept off his shoes, and then raked the food into a pile so I could dump it in the trash bag.

The entire time I worked, Richard couldn't stop apologizing. He knew this wasn't an enjoyable process, and he hated me having to do it. He would've much rather eaten a pleasant meal with me than sit in the middle of a crowded restaurant being mopped. As awkward as it was for me, it was worse for him. I was merely the janitor—he was the mess at which everyone gawked. He hadn't done it intentionally; he was just trying to eat lunch like the rest of them. But cerebral palsy rarely cooperated with Richard's designs.

It was this type of public fiasco that made me reevaluate the upside of our interminable, tedious school sessions, and pushed Richard to Julie's. Julie's Fresh Kitchen was a local diner/Mom and Pop restaurant that Richard began frequenting when his friend, Jody, opened it. Jody named it after his adopted daughter, and it quickly became our second home. This was the one place we went where Richard could be as loud and as messy as he wanted and neither one of us really cared because Jody and Amy, the waitress who always served Richard, were so gracious, hospitable, and thoughtful. Jody generously gave Richard one free meal a day for years, while also counseling him through the latest crises. He was more like a brother to Richard than another store proprietor.

Amy was one of the nicest, friendliest people walking the planet. Despite juggling numerous tables and customers, ringing people up, training new staff, and darting back and forth to the kitchen (she should've worn a track suit), she continually smiled, didn't complain, and took time to cut up Richard's salads into tiny pieces so it was easier for him to eat with the soup spoon she made sure we had. She waited patiently listening to Richard's slurred speech in the midst of a noisy restaurant with orders piling up because she knew he trusted her and confided in her and that these few moments with her and Jody were invaluable and irreplaceable.

Amy became like a sister to me. We bonded over our love of tennis, and though she was a diehard Roger Federer fan and I a loyal supporter of Rafael Nadal (I tried in vain to sway her opinion), we still managed to tease each other good-naturedly, which was a lot more than my three older brothers, dad, and I accomplished in the sports arena.

Maybe Mom should've banned sports from our home, though we undoubtedly could've found other things to argue about.

Amy was one of those rare people who saw the positive side to everything long before she noticed the drawbacks. She was more than an optimist, she was a possimist: Everything was possible, all plans doable, hope alive and well and thriving. She embodied the Pollyanna principle. Visiting her at Julie's was like stepping into Willy Wonka's Chocolate Factory, where wildest fantasies were realized and an after-dinner mint tasted like cherries jubilee.

She remembered the small things, too: a test Richard had coming up, Michael's birthday, Della's new shift at Chick-fil-A. I had no idea how Amy filed it all away between her customers' orders, her manager's requests, and her own family's lives, yet she balanced it perfectly like the three plates of food on her arm. She was a smiling, encouraging computer.

The end of lunch at Julie's was the saddest part of the day for Richard and me. It meant trekking home for more schoolwork, or haggling with store managers for deals, or potentially awkward, trying situations crouching just around the corner. Julie's was a safe haven, like flying home for the holidays for an hour each day. We sat back in our recliners devouring bowls of buttered popcorn while watching *A Christmas Carol*, as the tree blinked over in the corner and the turkey roasted in the oven. All that was missing was the presents, though I wouldn't have been surprised if Amy was in the back wrapping them.

CHAPTER TWELVE

The Bottom of the Unknown

One of the fiercest challenges facing any band was repetition. The willingness—much less the desire—to play the same songs over and over in rehearsals and gigs factored deeply into longevity. Two things broke up a band: egos and boredom.

And Yoko Ono, or other divisive love interests.

Drugs and booze, too.

Differences in musical direction.

A musician's growth impeded by bandmates' slower development.

Marriages and kids.

Apparently, lots of things broke up a band.

Anyway, boredom was definitely one of them. Don Henley once said he was blessed with a high tolerance for repetition, and it was essential for a career in music. Though we'd heard and practiced our songs two hundred times, various audience members at our shows were listening to them for their first. We had to be willing to play each tune like it was still a new song we were eager to share.

However, we also needed to write new material to progress as songwriters.

It was a slippery slope that Bryan, Manya, and I all had to navigate individually and collectively. It wasn't easy. Manya preferred focusing on new material for the creative challenge, I liked to hone a song until all of its potential was squeezed out, and Bryan bounced between both. It felt like we were driving a car five feet, shutting off the engine, cranking it up, and then driving another five feet in a big circle. It was difficult not to get on each other's nerves, and what frustrated me most was the quantity of songs for set lists. When we scrapped older songs for newer ones, we couldn't add length to our shows. Instead of being able to play for an hour and a half with extra material, we were stuck at forty-five minutes with one set. We couldn't book a gig for multiple sets without playing the same songs twice, which wasn't allowed unless the crowd was dragged out and replaced while we took five.

Also, when we went into the studio to record our full-length album, by the time we finished it six months later, some of the songs had grown stale and were dropped from our set list. I said, "How can we drop these songs? They're on our *album.*" Out with the old, in with the new.

Yet I didn't complain too loudly because we had Manya, whose voice was worth any headache, hindrance, or hassle. It reminded me of a cross between Chan Marshall of Cat Power and Regina Spektor, with a dash of Manya's own flair. She was barely five feet tall and a hundred pounds, yet an enormous voice twice her size boomed from her tiny mouth. It sounded like a radio clicked on blasting a mastered cut. Her technique, pitch, and control were flawless. She was already on the professional level, she just didn't realize it. If somebody had been able to convince her, we would've read about her in *Rolling Stone.*

After we self-released our album, a friend of Manya's with a local radio show wrote a positive review in the paper and invited us to play a few songs live during an on-air interview. It was an excellent opportunity for heightened exposure, so we quickly agreed. We had to make the most of this chance and capitalize on the momentum, so we agonized over which three songs to perform, rehearsed them countless times, wrote and rewrote lists of potential questions with amusing yet informative answers, and practiced the entire affair in Manya's garage like it was the actual interview. Bryan and I took turns as the host.

All of this for a twenty-minute interview on a college radio station. But we'd heard we should play to a crowd of four like they were four hundred, so we were thinking big.

On the night of the show, Bryan drove us all in our station wagon. I made the mistake of sitting in the backseat, the gentlemanly gesture so Manya could sit up front, yet a bad idea for my motion sickness. I got carsick extremely easily if I wasn't seated in the front, especially when Bryan got lost in a parking garage on campus and made about twenty-seven turns until he stumbled his way out. By the time we reached the station, my head hung out the window about to erupt.

I couldn't even help unload equipment. I crashed on a bench outside the radio station trying not to puke all over myself. Bryan and Manya took turns checking on me, tactfully inquiring if I felt up to staggering inside to play a few songs. We were on in five minutes.

I gave them the thumbs-up sign and dragged myself inside.

Thankfully, Manya did most of the talking and I didn't vomit on anything. Bryan played well and gave a few humorous answers, too. He'd made strides with his self-confidence, growing stronger after the practicum denial. He'd finished the fall semester with good grades and seemed motivated for the new year. I hoped he'd finally turned the corner.

Yet I also worried that too much of his optimism rode on the band. He was the type of person who stayed driven as long as a dream dangled in front of him. It didn't matter how far-fetched the aspiration, just that he felt he was making progress toward it. Our songs were on the radio (albeit a locals-only show), we'd recorded a demo and an album (without selling nearly enough copies yet to break even), we had band shirts (a box sat in my room), and we were playing shows (four or five gigs a month to half-filled rooms if we were lucky). I knew that to make real progress, we had to do more—a lot more. We needed to play ten to fifteen shows a month, even if it was Manya by herself doing open-mics. It was all exposure for the band. Bryan and I would have to move to Dallas so we could network and make the type of connections that opened doors. Hanging out at clubs getting to know other bands was just as important as practicing parts. We also needed to find a full-time drummer and a bassist (we'd done a few shows with different musicians, but nothing permanent) so we could flesh out our sound. We needed to find a manager we could trust who believed in us. And we had to be prepared to go on the road.

But I knew none of this would happen.

Manya had a daughter and couldn't roam across the country with an unknown band trying to win fans. It would've been different if we were a signed act with major-label backing on a real tour with actual buses, staff, and hotels without letters missing on their signs. But that was years away, if ever. Even if a local indie record label picked us up, it'd be bare bones for quite a while. Bryan couldn't drop out of school for that, not halfway to his master's. His parents would've sawed off his arms, and then mine.

I was the only one of us actually in a position to make such a radical commitment, and that wasn't nearly enough. Besides, I had goals left to reach with Richard, and a few more laps with Bryan at school, and a new relationship with Leslie to cultivate. I didn't want to abandon all of that to hop back in the van for more peanut butter.

Yet the band played on, partly to keep Bryan going, partly because I understood this would be my last musical hurrah, and partly because we were good. It was hard to give that up. But I knew we'd have to. I just didn't realize how soon.

"Put on my blue suede shoes and I boarded the plane. Touched down in the land of the Delta Blues in the middle of the pouring rain." I actually listened to Marc Cohn's song "Walking in Memphis" during my flight to meet Leslie for the first time. For years, I'd wondered what a "beal" was in the line, "Walking with my feet ten feet off of Beale." I'd never seen the lyrics, so I didn't realize it was a street, much less the most famous one in town home to legendary blues clubs and the Beale Street Flippers. I thought it was something similar to a banana peel that he'd slipped on, shooting him ten feet in the air. That didn't make a whole lot of sense, yet I pictured Cohn flying through the air every time I heard the song. Beale Street worked much better.

I also listened to America's "Daisy Jane," with its opening lines, "Flyin' me back to Memphis, gotta find my Daisy Jane." Others in the rotation included Paul Simon's "Graceland," Chuck Berry's "Back to Memphis," and "Maybe It Was Memphis" by Pam Tillis. As I listened, I skimmed William Patton's *A Guide to Historic Downtown Memphis* and G. Wayne Dowdy's *Hidden History of Memphis.* It wasn't that long of a flight from DFW to Memphis International Airport, so I didn't have much time to become an expert on Leslie's hometown. Yet I was determined to impress her, and her family, with *something* I'd gleaned. Basically, I wanted to sound like I knew what I was talking about even though I didn't.

After speaking on the phone for a few weeks, Leslie had invited me to Memphis to spend the weekend with her and her family. She emphasized that she wouldn't be offended if I couldn't come because of other plans or insufficient notice or a tonsillectomy or anything else that might take priority over meeting her. She definitely bent over backward never to impose or make me feel uncomfortable, which I greatly appreciated. However, I wanted to meet her in person. It was time—we'd been writing and talking for months. We'd both canceled our memberships to the dating site. We were pushing forward together. This was the logical, necessary next step.

Yet a tonsillectomy sounded a lot safer.

When we landed and I disembarked the plane, our pilot thanked me for flying with them. I wanted to ask him to take another trip around the block just to stall the inevitable. I was panicking. This was a bad idea. What was I doing here? I wasn't relationship material. I was a loner who rented rooms around the country while writing songs and books no one bought. Leslie's family would think she was pathetically desperate. *This guy, really? You sure you don't want to renew your membership? Maybe there's an ex-con who just joined.*

As I walked through the airport to meet Leslie, I saw a bathroom and debated hiding in one of the stalls until she gave up and left. *Tell her I missed the plane,* I schemed. *Tell her the plane crashed.* My thinking wasn't its razor sharpest, especially since I'd already texted her I'd landed safely. Plus, if we'd crashed, I'd be dead. But I still left it on the table as an option.

I felt like I'd pried open a container of cobras and couldn't reseal it. I was certain I'd end up hurting Leslie and it wasn't fair and it was out of my hands. The longer I continued with this charade, the deeper her feelings, and mine, would intensify, resulting in far worse agony than if I just folded now. I couldn't pull this off. I wasn't what she, or anyone, needed. I didn't know anything about stocks, IRAs, mortgages, landscaping, rewiring, wallpapering, or anything else related to being a husband and father. Leslie dreamed of owning a farm. The only thing I knew about farming was what I'd seen in the movie *Witness* with Harrison Ford, and somebody suffocated in a corn silo at the end of it, so I wasn't too keen on signing up. I was ready to give in and walk away.

But one thing stopped me, or more accurately, one person: Richard. I couldn't deny my time with him had been more beneficial than I ever could've imagined when we'd first met. If I'd followed my instinct to bolt, I would've missed out on all the great experiences we'd shared. My gut was no guide. Also, working with Richard had forced me to open up emotionally and become more verbally expressive of what was going on inside. People weren't mind readers, and sometimes they needed to hear what only I had to offer, regardless of how insignificant I viewed it. Lastly, one of the most invaluable lessons I'd learned from Richard involved joy. He took it where he could find it and reveled in it while it lasted. He didn't sit around worrying it would slip away or regret it if it finally did. He simply embraced happiness with all he had while he could without wasting a second.

There was a chance, possibly a strong one, I'd end up disappointing both Leslie and myself if I pursued this. Yet I enjoyed being with her, and I was thankful I'd met her. She made me laugh, and I somehow made her happy. That was worth holding onto as long as we could.

She was just up ahead. I saw a small crowd of people smiling and waving at my fellow passengers as we trudged closer, one holding a poster that read HAPPY BIRTHDAY, LAURA!!! Leslie was somewhere in there. At first, I couldn't find her because she was only five feet, three inches tall. She also hated drawing attention to herself, so she wouldn't be flapping a poster. More likely, she was ducking behind someone waiting to snare me as I wandered by.

The birthday girl, Laura, was ahead of me, because she started hugging the woman clutching the poster and then the burly man next to her. Either they were her folks or she was ecstatic to be in Memphis. Maybe she'd had a round or two on the plane. Maybe I should've. All three of them walked off together, revealing Leslie.

It felt like a scene in a movie, except when I walked up to her, I held out my hand to shake. Was she my new business partner? A handshake? What was I thinking? I really stunk at this.

Thankfully, Leslie smiled and hugged me, correctly chalking it up to nerves. Yet that was only the beginning of my blunders. As we walked out of the airport, I couldn't zip up my coat. It was chilly outside and I wanted to stay warm, but I couldn't get the infernal zipper to work. My mom had once proclaimed her strong preference for snaps over zippers and buttons and, clearly, she was right again. I needed to push beyond snaps to an entire outfit made with Velcro. I finally stopped just before reaching the automatic sliding doors, put down my bags, and went to war with that little zipper, yanking on it like a maniac until it caved in and zipped. I looked at Leslie who was doubled over laughing, thoroughly amused by the show, which was a much more positive reaction than I got from the people hustling passed. They looked like they were ready to flag down TSA.

Leslie drove me to the Booksellers at Laurelwood, a large bookstore with an extensive variety of works, including a thorough children's section and a bistro. It was here we had our first meal together—our first "date"—and I finally got to put a live face with the words I'd been hearing and reading for months. I'd seen pictures of Leslie, but one-dimensional representations offered only so much information. They didn't come close to conveying the warmth I felt in her smile, the adoration I saw in her brown eyes, the unmasked joy on her beautiful face. For some bizarre reason, she looked thrilled that I was sitting across from her in one of her favorite hometown nooks, the waiting and anticipation finally over. I was real and this was actually happening and she could touch me, which she now did as she reached over to hold my hand. We were together, and it felt like a lifetime ago that I'd considered looking into a dating site. It was strange how the force of a relationship skewed time. Perspective and priorities realigned to leave enough room for the continent charging downstream. All else waited its turn.

A year ago, I never would've gotten on the plane.

Something had changed in me. Initially, I dismissed it as fear of winding up alone. I was merely desperate, flailing my arms out here in the bottomless unknown for anything that might keep me afloat, my broken boat long out of view. Yet there was an undeniable yearning I couldn't pretend away, and putting someone else first had sparked it. Once I started placing others' needs above mine, my little boat wasn't big enough. I needed space to receive encouragement, to learn to accept it as unconditionally as it was offered. And to tell others how I felt. To make sure they understood their importance to me. It was the hardest thing I'd ever done, but the alternative wasn't enough anymore. The process had begun and couldn't be reversed. I was transitioning or, more accurately, sinking all the way to the bottom because I had to know what awaited me. Just like Richard, not knowing wasn't acceptable. I had to find out who was down there, tucked behind a rock, and where she might lead.

CHAPTER THIRTEEN

How to Hold a Fork

When I returned from Memphis, Richard wanted to know everything that had happened, what Leslie's family was like, where we went, when I was getting married.

"What?" I exclaimed. "Married? I just visited her for the first time."

He laughed, and said, "Look at me and Della. Slow poke."

"You guys floored it in the express lane. I drive the speed limit."

"You need me to chaperone you two?"

"No, thanks. You'd steer us straight to church for the ceremony."

He laughed even harder, followed by coughing and sweet tea. Then he said, "I could do it myself. I'm a reverend."

I smiled while nodding. "You charge too much."

"I'll give you a discount."

"What can you do for me?" I couldn't resist using his line.

At that, we both cracked up.

Richard's topic of marriage felt highly premature, yet it did make me wonder if he worried about me leaving. At some point, I would. It was inevitable. We weren't going to spend the rest of our lives together. I didn't think. I was learning not to jump to assumptions, so I tried to remain open on all fronts.

So far, Richard had been unsuccessful in finding a suitable replacement for Troy. One dog a friend had trained couldn't perform all the necessary tasks, while another pooch we found through a local instructor grew defensive any time someone approached Richard. We wanted a service dog, not a bodyguard. As disappointing as these results were for Richard, it did allow us more time alone. When Troy was still here, Richard tended to focus on him, especially when we were out in public. But now it was just us, and as unlikely as I would've imagined it at the beginning, I'd come to enjoy hanging out with Richard. Our bond had deepened over these last several months. Often, it felt like I aided him the most with companionship. More than school, letters, errands, or whatever else we did, having me around all day to talk to and to joke with seemed to lift his spirits. He wasn't in this alone. I completely understood I'd never provide the type of love, fulfillment, and affirmation Della introduced into his life, or that Michael and his kids gave. They were on another level I couldn't touch.

But I could be Richard's buddy. I doubted he'd ever had one, at least not without emotional strings attached. When was the last time someone other than Della spent the day with Richard just to have fun? Not because it was the right thing to do, but the most desirable choice? My employment excluded me from this list. I had to be with him. Yet the longer I spent my days driving him around and feeding him chicken salad and tea, the more I missed him on weekends when I was free to do what I wanted. He made me laugh, which had risen nearly to the top of my character-traits heap. Someone with a good sense of humor and a positive outlook simply made life more enjoyable, and with disillusionment constantly angling for a clean shot, friends like Richard became priceless. If I had to help him take a drink to get to be around that kind of optimism, so be it. A small cost to plunk down. I was still cleaning up.

One Saturday that spring semester, I took Bryan to school for a special conference, and while running errands I stopped by Richard's house to see what he was doing. The kids were at friends' houses, and he and Della had just popped in the movie *Hachi* and invited me to join them. So I did. Della deep-fried some French fries in peanut oil, easily the best I ever had. I asked her why she hadn't cooked these before, and she said, "Because we'd all weigh twenty pounds more."

It felt different being in Richard's home without punching the time clock, like I was cheating. I sat back on the couch halfway expecting him to start dictating an email. Yet he just settled in for the movie, content to have me along for the ride, and it was one emotional rollercoaster.

Hachi starred Richard Gere, Joan Allen, and a dog, which wasn't a shocker. Richard loved any movie or TV show with dogs. They were almost prerequisites. Except for *Walker, Texas Ranger*, his favorite show, but that had Chuck Norris, who was equal to a kennel of highly trained service dogs plus a year's supply of treats. He was probably half-canine.

Gere's character, Professor Wilson, found an Akita puppy at the train station, took him home, and fell in love with the little guy. Ken, a Japanese professor friend, translated a symbol on the puppy's collar for the number eight—"Hachi" in Japanese—that signified good fortune, so Wilson chose that for his name. The pup wouldn't play traditional games like fetch or chase, but he did enjoy following Wilson to the train station each morning to see him off and then greeting him at the station when he returned from college. One day, Wilson died during a lecture and, obviously, didn't come home, much to the confusion and disappointment of Hachi, who continued waiting until Wilson's son-in-law collected him. Unsatisfied with this result, Hachi returned to the train station each day to wait for his beloved owner.

Finally, Wilson's wife, Cate, sold their house and moved away, giving Hachi to her daughter. Again, this didn't work for Hachi, who escaped and found his way back to the train station where he'd last seen Wilson. He slept in a rail yard at night, while waiting at the station all day. Friends of Wilson's who worked at the station remembered Hachi and fed him and tried to watch out for him the best they could. An article was written about Hachi in the local paper. Ken read the article and visited Hachi. Cate returned home to visit her husband's grave on the tenth anniversary of his death and ran into Ken, who told her about Hachi. She went to the train station and was stunned to find an old Hachi still staring at the doors waiting patiently for his owner to walk out. Crying and distraught, she sat next to Hachi until the next train arrived.

After she left, Hachi continued waiting, day after day, until he finally died in the snow, cold and alone.

Della looked at Richard, who was sobbing his eyes out, and then she turned to me and joked, "Is he going to make it?" But I was falling apart, too. "Are *you*?"

I shook my head and whimpered, "Thanks for the fun movie. I feel so much better."

Hanging out at Richard's was more dangerous than I realized.

It took us a few minutes to pull ourselves together. Between sniffles and sponging tears, Richard graciously offered me the hand towel hooked to his lanyard (alongside his cellphone) that he coughed into all day, yet I opted for a quick trip to the bathroom. It was especially tough for Richard with Troy being gone and no replacement found. He loved his pooches. I thought it was a sweet movie about unconditional loyalty and love, but it needed to come with a warning that an entire box of Kleenex would be used during viewing.

A few weekends later, we tried animals in a different, happier setting: the zoo. Of course, when I told Leslie where I was headed, she launched into a tirade about the cruelty of dragging animals out of their natural habitats to cage them for entertainment. Just when I thought it was safe to return to the animal kingdom, more depression awaited.

I accompanied Richard, Della, and their kids to the Fort Worth Zoo, secretly looking forward to seeing hippos, elephants, tigers, gorillas, and lions. I couldn't afford to travel on safari to Africa, and just once I wanted to see them in person. I'd been to the zoo when I was a little kid, but I couldn't recall anything other than my dad arguing with the ticket guy at the window (I later learned it was over a group discount no longer offered).

Richard's favorite animal was the lion, followed closely by the elephant. He liked the fact that humans could train them by establishing a bond. The connection between man and animal was the key aspect for him. It went back to his many years handling service dogs. He was interested in the other animals, taking time to stop and observe their routines and movements and to read each placard. He liked the penguins a lot, as did we all. Who didn't love penguins? Yet when we reached the lions, Richard became almost entranced, staring at the two powerful beasts perched on their rocks overlooking the zoo like they, indeed, were in charge of the jungle, wherever relocated. Della and I sensed Richard wanted his space, so we drifted a ways off, while the kids took selfies and the passersby chatted, munched popcorn, or snapped their own keepsakes.

It looked like Richard was trying to hypnotize the lions. He wouldn't take his eyes off them. It reminded me of when he read a textbook as Computer Lady called out the highlighted words on the screen. I whispered to Della, "What's he doing?"

"Training them," she said quietly.

I quipped, "Doesn't he need a whip and a chair?"

I was being half-serious, yet she merely rolled her eyes and said, "Ha ha." From the look on my perplexed face, she could tell I required further clarification, so she explained, "In his mind. He likes to watch them and train them in his mind. Same with elephants. It's why he likes the circus so much. He goes in the back to meet the trainers, learn all he can."

"But…but how does he train them from this side of the fence thirty feet away? Telepathy?"

"You played sports, right?" she said, sounding much like my mom. "What was the first thing your coach did?"

"Called me the wrong name."

She giggled and said, "Before that. Did he try to get everyone's attention so you and your teammates focused on him?"

I nodded.

"There you go. The first step in connecting with an animal, as I understand it, is to capture its attention. Get it to focus on you."

"Preferably without waving meat," I suggested.

"Definitely. If Richard can feel like he's captured the lions' attention just through eye contact, he'll be happy. He'll feel like he made a connection."

I watched Richard for a few moments, as Emilee asked her mom to take a picture of Evelyn and her with one of the lions in the background. Michael didn't get to be in the photo, but little brothers rarely did. Besides, he seemed content eating the nachos left over from lunch. I studied both lions for any movement toward Richard. Right now, they were both looking away from him, more in the direction of Michael's nachos, which was understandable. Richard kept staring at them, though the lions didn't flinch. But as Della wrapped up the photo session with her girls, one of the lions turned slightly toward Richard, who was glaring so intently he looked like he was about to fire laser beams out of his eyes. The lion turned a little more, yet still not quite at Richard. I almost screamed, *Keep going!*

Della rejoined me, and we watched in silence for almost a minute with no more progress. It seemed that was as far as the lion deigned to shift his gaze. The kids were growing antsy to move on. Della corralled them, while I went to retrieve Richard.

But on my way over, it happened. The king of the jungle turned his head so he was looking straight at Richard, squarely into his eyes, and I froze. For the next twenty or thirty seconds, Richard and the lion refused to take their eyes off each other, introducing themselves the only way they could. I wanted to tell the crowd to be quiet, something important was happening over here, yet it didn't seem to bother the two of them. Richard and his lion were locked on each other like they were physically incapable of snapping the spell.

Finally, a family nearby began laughing loudly, and the lion looked away. Richard turned his chair and approached me. I wasn't sure if it was appropriate, but I couldn't help myself and I asked him, "Did you make contact?"

"Like you wouldn't believe," he answered, before catching up to Della and the girls. I looked back at the lion, yet he'd put his head down, presumably for a nap. He seemed tired from his connection with Richard. I completely understood. This emotional bonding stuff was hard work.

My first visit to Memphis had gone as well as I could've hoped, aside from my nervous blunders. I met Leslie's family at El Chico, their favorite restaurant. Before we walked into the restaurant, Leslie introduced me to her mom in the parking lot. The first thing I (and most people) noticed was her white hair, though she was only in her mid-fifties. The second thing I noted was where Leslie got her thoughtfulness and kindness. Her mom greeted me like we were old friends, instantly knocking some of the weight off my shoulders.

Leslie's family had been coming to El Chico for over thirty years since her parents had dated. It was the only one in town. They told lots of hilarious tales of a three-year-old Leslie shocking the manager by asking for a bowl of jalapeños, a very young family friend hiding under the table because she was scared of the waiters singing "Happy Birthday" to her, Leslie's mom terrified the kids would all get lice from wearing the same sombrero. I was in stitches.

I took mental notes, trying to learn all I could about Leslie's family (more cramming for my imaginary final exam). Her brother, Joey, reminded me of my oldest brother, Andy, in that he was naturally talented and seemed to know something about everything. He was also a great storyteller. Leslie's sister, Emily, was down to earth and extremely easy to talk to, which helped me tremendously. I needed slow-pitch softballs, not fastballs, in conversations. Her youngest sister, Elisabeth, was a budding singer and just as friendly and considerate as Leslie and her mom. Joey and his wife, Dorothy, had an adorable baby girl, Julia. Dorothy was pleasant and quiet, which may have been the greatest aid to me because I wasn't the only one at the table not saying much. They were all adept at speak-screaming over one another, undoubtedly from years of experience. In contrast, my family chose to avoid talking to each other to spare the effort.

Leslie's dad was the ringleader and by far the loudest. He was a skilled glazer who had installed much of the glass in the downtown buildings. He was smart, opinionated, curious, slightly deaf, and harmless. For a Vietnam veteran who built their new house out in Brighton (forty-five minutes from midtown) by himself over sixteen years of weekends, he was as tender and encouraging as they came. His thick, rough, tanned hands looked like they could snap my left leg in half, yet he made me feel welcomed and included. He asked plenty of questions about my family, job, band, and even Bryan, whom Leslie had told them about. By the end of lunch, I felt comfortable around them all, especially Leslie's mom. Per my personal motto, I'd hoped for the best and expected the worst. I was relieved to be wrong again.

When it was time to leave, Leslie's family revealed another distinctive practice totally opposite of my family's traditional exit. When the meal was done at our house, we fled in different directions as fast as possible like a homicide had just taken place. But Leslie's family liked to hug it out. I got a warm embrace from every member present, minus Joey, who opted for a handshake, for which I was grateful. I'd just received more hugs in a two-minute span than during my entire upbringing; one more might've sent me into seizures.

We made lots of stops that weekend. Leslie took me downtown for a personal sightseeing tour, all the while pointing out various buildings her dad had helped build. He'd gotten around. We went to the grand Peabody Memphis Hotel and saw the famous Peabody Ducks that lived on the hotel rooftop and made daily strolls through the lobby. When we went to the roof, I remembered the scene from *The Firm* in which Tom Cruise threatened to hurl himself over the edge because of his wife's concerns about his peculiar new coworkers. He should've listened.

We visited Beale Street where I (along with probably a hundred thousand tourists before me) sang the line, "Walking with my feet ten feet off of Beale" from Cohn's song. Leslie playfully placed her left thumb and index finger (she was a leftie) to her forehead in the shape of an "L" to indicate I'd stooped to cheesy tourist stunts only losers dared. Immediately, I sang Beck's, "I'm a loser, baby, so why don't you kill me?" She just rolled her eyes and dragged me into A. Schwab's before I could make a bigger scene.

She took me on a tour of Gibson's guitar factory, which I wished Bryan could've seen. Though he would've undoubtedly drawn way too much attention to our group by yelling "COOL!" every five feet. It was Christmas morning whenever he saw something new he liked.

We rode on a trolley through downtown Memphis, toured Sun Studios, where I relived the scene from U2's *Rattle and Hum* rockumentary when they recorded "Angel of Harlem," wrote our names on the wall outside Graceland (no Elvis sightings), played a round of putt-putt (this became a tradition), and ate dinner at Leslie's personal favorite, The Beauty Shop. Long ago, it was called Atkins Beauty and Barber Shop, where Priscilla Presley got her hair done. The original cone-shaped hair dryers were still in place, along with the avocado green salon sinks behind the bar. The delicious dessert menu was written on a huge mirror, and tables were made from the old salon seats. It was simultaneously vintage, hip, and fun, with scrumptious-looking dishes like Pan-roasted Barramundi, Maple-glazed Benton's Bacon-wrapped Steak Frites, and Shrimp a la Plancha and Grilled Avocado. I could see why it was so popular.

After we were seated, it was time to put all my training and research to use. This was a special place to Leslie, and I felt the significance. Yet I was prepared. One dinner before I left, Bryan's dad had politely suggested I consider adjusting my grip on my utensils. Apparently, I clutched them like a caveman trying to kill my food before it wiggled away. He demonstrated the proper underhanded grip, which seemed to offer much less control yet was the more refined, socially accepted technique. He said, "Trust me: You don't want to hold your fork like a baseball bat in front of Leslie." I thanked him for the advice, clearly in need of as much sound counsel as I could get.

I'd also recalled a tip my old youth pastor at our church in D.C. had tossed out one lunch. He was telling me about his courtship of his wife and how on their first dinner he devoured all of his food before she was even a third finished. After roughly forty seconds of silence, it dawned on him that he now had to carry the conversation for the rest of the meal. There was nothing else to do—he'd eaten his other options. He warned me, "When you go on a date, do *not* eat fast, or else you'll become the main attraction." Plus, it undoubtedly made the girl feel self-conscious to be the only one eating.

When our salads were served, I held my fork just as Bryan's dad had modeled and paced my comments so I wouldn't run out of things to say. I longed for the days when uncomfortable silence turned safe, but my insecurities weren't quite there yet.

I knew this was the perfect time to drop one of the historical nuggets about Memphis I'd learned from my books. I wanted to pick something Leslie wouldn't know, though she seemed pretty knowledgeable about the town in which she'd grown up. After a last-second mental coin toss, I went with the following: "Did you know that grocery shoppers used to give their lists to clerks who filled the orders? They weren't allowed to pick products by themselves. They had to wait in long lines at the counter while the clerks tracked down their items. Customers didn't even know the exact prices a lot of times and were overcharged. But when Clarence Saunders opened his first Piggly Wiggly here in Memphis, he let customers shop for themselves. They were free to walk wherever they wanted, with price tags above every product. The way we shop today started right here in Memphis."

I sat back to let Leslie absorb the power of the pearl I'd just unveiled. I doubted she'd visit her local market the same way again. I'd rocked her world—her silence was confirmation. It was a lot to take in. I gave her a moment to process. Then she coughed and took a drink of water, before apologizing, "Sorry, something went down wrong…Okay, all better. I know, isn't that neat?! That store was on Jefferson Avenue. There's a replica of it in the Pink Palace Museum near my house. I want to take you there."

So much for rocking her world.

I should've tried one of my other historical nuggets, though she probably knew those, too. She was one sharp cookie, much smarter than I. I returned to chewing my food slowly.

After dinner, we sat on a huge log by the Mississippi River with a stunning view of the brilliantly lit Hernando de Soto Bridge, named for the sixteenth-century Spanish explorer who scouted this portion of the Mississippi River, another fact I'd picked up from my reading. I said, "The Hernando de Soto Bridge sure is pretty," with heartfelt nods for emphasis.

Leslie chuckled, and replied, "You mean the New Bridge?"

"It's new?"

She shrugged and said, "Newer than the Memphis & Arkansas Bridge. Nobody here calls it that. Maybe the M Bridge because it's shaped like an M. But usually just the New Bridge."

"Oh. Interesting." More nodding.

"It's like Memphis State," she continued. "They changed its name back in '94 to the University of Memphis, but locals like my daddy still call it Memphis State. That's what he grew up calling it, so that's its name."

"Huh. I didn't know that." No more nuggets from my book. I was in over my head.

I looked at the water imagining Huck and Jim floating by on their raft down the Mighty Miss. It was gigantic. I would've thought twice before hopping on a makeshift raft to traverse this river. Of course, they hadn't much choice. I thought about mentioning to Leslie that it was the fourth-longest river in the world, passing through or bordering ten states. But I was sure she'd learned that long ago. She'd probably helped write my Memphis history books.

We walked for a bit along the river, holding hands in the idyllic setting. *I should kiss her,* I thought. *Now would be the perfect time. We're by the Mississippi River, for crying out loud. It won't get more romantic than this. Pull the trigger! Make your move!!*

But then I saw another couple ambling toward us, and my window for execution vanished. However, even if they hadn't appeared, I probably would've chickened out. I was an expert at it. Plus, Leslie was modest and making out in public undoubtedly wouldn't have appealed to her.

At least, that helped me justify waiting.

It was while watching a movie on her couch with her three dogs, Atticus, Bear, and Dill, surrounding us that our first kiss finally happened. Slim Dill was partly wedged between us, either jealous for attention or wanting to join in. Maybe a bit of both. Bear (who looked like one) slept near my feet by the air vent, while muscular Atti reclined on his soft bed near the TV. We were watching an intensely romantic, delicate, tear-jerking movie called *Superbad*, with Jonah Hill. Leslie had seen it and promised it was funny, which it was, but not really romantic date night material. More like frat house flick night. Yet it worked. Before we made it halfway through, Leslie, Dill, and I were kissing. I owed Mr. Hill one.

My trip to Memphis couldn't have gone better, but now the time had come for Leslie to visit me in electrifying Fort Worth. I worried she might fall asleep as soon as she hit town.

CHAPTER FOURTEEN

Under the Dog Pile

Richard's wheelchair took a pounding. It was beaten up, scratched, dented, and creaked as it rolled along with one wobbly wheel. It looked like it would collapse underneath him at any moment. He needed to wear a mini-parachute to break his fall. I kept waiting for the day either his chair or Big Blue (or both) broke down, stranding us for hours somewhere in the city.

Under Medicaid, Richard's wheelchair could be replaced only every five years, so he had to wait a little longer for a new one. That meant lots of trips to The Healthcare Store in Hurst about forty minutes away. It was a full-service shop providing a variety of medical equipment such as manual and power wheelchairs, scooters, lifts and ramps, and bath aids. They customized products for their customers, too, which was perfect for Richard because he usually wanted something adjusted on his chair in addition to the frequent maintenance required. John, the owner, was incredibly nice, generous, and patient, and he put up with Richard's hot-rodding around town with little more than gentle pleas to drive a little slower over the railroad tracks and speed bumps.

Despite the long round trip to Hurst, I enjoyed going to The Healthcare Store. All the employees and technicians were extremely friendly to Richard, which I appreciated. When he felt comfortable, I felt at ease. After Julie's, this was one of his favorite spots to visit, even though it meant his chair was struggling. There was no haggling and no language barrier. They all understood Richard or didn't mind listening a second time to ensure they heard him correctly. They genuinely seemed to care about helping people. It was one of those rare stores that actually lived out the maxim I found in its pamphlet that they'd treat everyone with the dignity and respect they deserved. This made it a joy to go there.

Plus, there was a bakery close by.

But Richard's chair wasn't the only thing taking a beating. Sometimes I thought Richard should wear a helmet. That orange light on top of his wheelchair wasn't nearly enough to alert motorists he was heading their way. Richard was accustomed to driving himself around—he'd done it his whole life. Even though he now had a van, he still liked to "walk," as he put it, whenever possible. Once, while on a scouting expedition for their new house, Richard explored a potential neighborhood and was hit by a car as he crossed an intersection. The driver never noticed him while making a U-turn. Richard was thrown twenty feet in the air, chair and all. I saw the accident from afar and sprinted to Richard sprawled on his side in the middle of the street with his chair still glued to his back. His seat belt meant business—they must've used them on rocket ships.

I lay down on the street to see how badly Richard was hurt. Miraculously, he smiled at me, and said, "Hoowee. I don't know about this house."

If I hadn't been scared out of my mind, I would've broken down laughing hysterically. Only Richard would've said that then.

I glanced back at Della hurrying over, and before I stood up to meet her, Richard reminded, "Don't go too far."

I patted him on the arm, and said, "I'll be right here."

Somehow, Richard wasn't seriously injured other than a huge hematoma on his back from where his wheelchair had scraped him. His chair, though, needed major repairs. Fortunately, insurance covered it, and it gave us the perfect excuse to spend more time at The Healthcare Store.

As if that flight wasn't harrowing enough, Richard sailed through the air again shortly before Leslie visited. It happened one evening after I was already home. Della and Richard were in the parking lot of Hulen Mall getting ready to leave after her shift at Chick-fil-A. She raised Richard up on Big Blue's lift, with Richard facing away from the van. He always backed into the van off the lift because it was easier for him to position his chair to be lashed down. Just when he was about to begin backing in, his cellphone rang. Della reached up to answer it for him, but she accidentally bumped his chair's joystick, launching Richard forward off the lift face-first onto the pavement, his chair still dutifully hugging him. I was in awe of his seat belt.

Della immediately called the ambulance, and Richard ended up having to get stitches in his forehead. His left ankle was sore, yet he escaped major injury again. He was the true Man of Steel. I told him, "Maybe you should work at the circus as the guy who gets shot out of the canon. You could hang out with the elephants. You'd have a ball."

He laughed and said, "Your turn. I've done it."

Poor Della felt miserable over the accident. She'd merely tried to help Richard answer his phone so he didn't fumble for it up on the lift and risk injury, resulting in painful irony. Richard tried to ease her guilt the best he could, assuring her he wasn't mad and that many people had accidentally bumped his joystick through the years. It was easy to do. He said, "I'm fine, honey. The chair's okay. All's well that ends well."

Yet we weren't quite out of the woods.

The doctor diagnosed Richard's sore left ankle as sprained and added that it didn't really matter if it was sprained or broken because it was non-weight bearing. Easy for him to say. Richard insisted it was broken because the pain was killing him, yet it was logged as a sprain.

Over the next two weeks, Richard complained louder and louder about his ankle, yet I presumed he was simply having difficulty dealing with the soreness. Whenever Della was available, he begged her to massage his swollen ankle, and when she wasn't, he enlisted me. I didn't mind because he was clearly in a lot of discomfort, though once when he asked me to do it in a very public place, I wished we could return to the halcyon days of desperate bathroom dashes.

Depending on Della's shift, we visited her every so often at Chick-fil-A. It didn't matter when we hit the mall's food court, Chick-fil-A was always the busiest eatery. I felt sorry for the bored employees standing behind the other counters envying the long lines stretched out before Della and her coworkers. I wanted to go order a lamb gyro or a bowl of wonton soup just to keep them company, yet I had to maintain loyalty to Della's employer. We were a Chick-fil-A family.

Of course, if I'd been in their shoes, I would've been grateful not to get mobbed all day. I'd seen Della when she stumbled home after an exhausting shift doling out waffle fries and chicken sandwiches. She could've used a few extended breaks.

Richard and I arrived at the food court early that morning, not long after Della's shift started. There was already a line of hungry shoppers salivating over chicken, egg, and cheese bagels, hash brown scramble burritos, and chicken biscuits smothered in Chick-fil-A Sauce (the best dipping sauce I ever tried). The other restaurants' employees might as well have played poker in the back—they certainly weren't needed out front.

I liked malls. Most people I asked didn't. Too many lines, noise, noise, noise, credit cards maxed, mental and physical exhaustion. But where I'd grown up in Oxon Hill, Maryland, we had only a strip mall, not a proper mall with two or three levels, a food court, major department stores like Macy's and Dillard's, Santa at Christmas, and maybe even an ice skating rink. The whole operation enclosed in one giant building like its own city separate from the one outside. It was as if I'd walked into another world, like a large resort hotel, except with soft pretzels and a movie theater. In the mornings or at lunch, people slipped on their sneakers to walk the mall like a free, air-conditioned gym. Parents arranged play dates for their kids with friends at the children's play zones. Concerts were given, cars raffled off, book signings held. There was never enough time to try everything, like vacationing in a foreign country with only two hours to explore. I usually wasn't ready to leave.

Except today.

Richard led us past the lines waiting at Chick-fil-A to the counter where Della stood smiling wearily. She was taking a customer's order, though the slender, older man didn't request any special sauce. *Big mistake,* I thought. *Go for the sauce. Add the dipping sauce!* He left it dry. A regrettable choice.

Richard tried to tell Della his ankle felt worse, yet her hands were full with ravenous customers who held no special sympathy for Richard's pain. They wanted to eat. Now. If Richard required a word with his wife, he'd have to mosey to the back of the line. It was somewhere near the parking lot.

Yet rather than hold out for his turn with Della, Richard had another idea. He pushed his joystick so that his chair reclined until he was fully horizontal. Then he looked at me while pointing at his left foot, and said, "Take my shoe off."

"Sorry?" I said, pretending I didn't understand what he'd asked or where this was headed.

"My shoe," he said more emphatically. "Take it off. And my sock."

We were right next to the counter at Chick-fil-A, with two lines of customers standing six to ten feet away. This wasn't happening. This was a terrible dream.

I glanced at Della, who shook her head but then shrugged as if to say, *No, not here...well, his mind's made up.*

I bent over and whispered in Richard's right ear, "Maybe we should do this outside."

He looked at me like he didn't care if the Royal Family was having tea at the next table, he was in pain. "Please rub my ankle," he asked in such a pathetic way that I would've had to surgically remove my heart and puree it to say no.

I stood up and slowly slid off his shoe, hoping by the time I reached his bare foot, security would intervene. I placed his soft, brown dress shoe with the Velcro strap by the side of his wheelchair nearest the customers, praying they'd put two and two together and flee while they still could. Things were about to get weird.

I peeled off Richard's black dress sock as gradually as possible to give all present one last warning before showtime. It felt like

I was doing a striptease. Richard typically wore socks only in the dead of winter, but it was much cooler today than yesterday. Fort Worth's weather was a meteorological yo-yo—one day it was seventy degrees, the next thirty-five. Every day I packed extra clothes in the morning like I was traveling abroad.

Richard's ankle was badly swollen. Nobody wanted to see it while scarfing down a bacon, egg, and cheese biscuit. I didn't want to see it. It looked lifeless, like a bloated mannequin's leg. I fought the urge to rip off my coat and lay it over his ankle in respect for the dead.

I looked at Della one more time for an eleventh-hour reprieve from the governor, yet she'd turned to fill a drink order. She probably couldn't bear to watch. *Who wants drinks? I'll fill 'em. I got it. Who needs something from the back? Let me do it!* I was surprised she didn't stoop down to look for more straws under the counter never to resurface.

So I began massaging Richard's ankle. Each time I rubbed, he bit his right hand due to the pain. "Do you want me to stop?" I asked hopefully.

He merely shook his head while grimacing.

The customers in line didn't know what to make of this. It was like a carnival freak show had just pulled up. They couldn't take their stunned, perplexed eyes off us. Some of them were whispering to each other. Perhaps they wondered when one of us would swallow a sword.

I kept rubbing Richard's swollen ankle, unsure if I was helping or hurting him. Each second that passed was more embarrassing than the last. I was standing in the middle of a mall massaging Richard's swollen ankle in front of a shocked crowd. *For the love of God, do they not have security cameras in this place? Does anything go here? We might as well clean out the cash drawer before we leave.*

Finally, Richard groaned, "Okay, stop. That's enough." My hands popped off his ankle like I'd touched a hot oven rack. I grabbed his sock from inside his shoe and slid it on as quickly as possible without hurting him, and then wiggled on his shoe as he bit his hand some more. I wanted to apologize to the folks waiting in line, but the damage was done. These images were permanently seared into their memories. It would've been more appropriate to hug them and say good luck.

Richard returned his chair to its normal upright position, and we took our leave. Our work here was done. I doubted the manager of Chick-fil-A would be inviting us back anytime soon. In fact, I hoped Della pretended she didn't know us to protect her job.

Not long after the massage, Della did leave Chick-fil-A to work at a daycare facility just down the street from their house. She said it had nothing to do with our little stunt, simply a more convenient job. She could come home for lunch, check on Richard, etc. I was happy she could be closer to home, though I did worry about the kids she was watching. They couldn't handle a repeat performance of what we did in the mall. They'd have nightmares for years. Della's boss needed to bar the front door if she saw Richard and me coming.

After a few weeks of torture, Richard went to a chiropractor who said his ankle was broken in two places. The doctor he'd seen after the accident needed to have his license revoked. I felt guilty for presuming Richard was merely having difficulty coping with the soreness of a sprained ankle. If my ankle was broken in two places, I would've griped and moaned all day while crying like a baby. In hindsight, he'd handled it admirably.

For the next few months, Richard visited the chiropractor to have electrical muscle stimulation treatments done on his ankle.

They attached electrodes to his ankle that were connected to a device with a timer that beeped when he was done, like a frozen dinner in the microwave. One day as he lay on the table for treatment, he said to me, grinning, "Next time you'll believe me, won't you?"

I answered, "Next time we'll get a second opinion. And a third." Anything to prevent more public massages.

Leslie and I talked on the phone each night, while I continued to write her as many letters as possible. I knew the more I could write instead of speak, the better off I'd be. It was harder to find time to write—and things to mention—because we were talking on the phone every day. I had to dig deep to uncover something to write about other than last night's sudden rain shower, but it helped me learn to express what was buried in my head.

When we talked, I remembered a piece of advice Richard had given me. He and I were joking around one day after posting an assignment, and when we finished laughing, he grew more serious and said, "Just keep this in mind: Sarcasm's like dynamite."

"Huh? Where'd that come from?"

"It's true. Especially on the phone, long distance. Be careful with that." He shook his head as if recalling a bad experience, before adding, "Things get misunderstood real fast when you're not in person. They jump to conclusions and hang up before you can fix it. Gets worse the longer you leave it."

I leaned forward, taking more mental notes. This was important. I asked, "Did this happen with you and Della?"

"Not just Della," he said, sighing. "Lots of folks. I'm a slow learner."

"What if I say I was just joking? You know, make sure she

understands I'm kidding around."

Richard responded with something I thought about for years to come. He said, "Next time you have a big argument, go back to where it started. All the way to the beginning. Bet it was a sarcastic joke. They're like little cracks in a dam."

It was a great insight to remember when talking to Leslie (or anyone). A seemingly innocent bit of sarcasm could easily lead to more biting sarcasm that opened the door to hurt feelings and resentment and picking at one another and insults and before long a confrontation and finally a shouting match. All from one sarcastic jab. That was a treacherous road to travel over the phone, and often how relationships ended. I decided any joke with Leslie that carried an ounce of derision was off-limits. It wasn't worth the risk. It probably saved us countless fights, possibly even a breakup, and for that, I owed Richard big.

Long-distance relationships were tricky. It was a marathon, not a sprint, requiring water stations and carbohydrates along the way to avoid giving up. Leslie and I had to make progress without seeing each other for long stretches. It was easy to feel disappointed and dispirited. We couldn't simply hang out, so we had to make up for the absence. To do this, we tried to share daily life as much as possible through texts, calls, and letters. I told her the latest with the band and how Bryan was faring. I played her new songs I was working on, even softly strumming the guitar over the phone many nights until she fell asleep. She told me about the cases she'd worked on, the new additions her dad had completed on their house in Brighton, how Dill and Bear were getting along (they had a sibling rivalry for a while).

We watched *The Office* together on the phone every Thursday night. Though the show had already aired for several seasons, I'd never seen it. Leslie convinced me it was hilarious and even sent me DVDs of all the seasons I'd missed. She was right—I couldn't stop laughing. We howled over Jim moving Dwight's desk to the men's bathroom, Michael defining the word "wedding" on Phyllis's big day as "the fusing of two metals with a hot torch," Kevin spilling a tub of his famous chili on the carpet and then falling in it, Stanley professing his undying love for Pretzel Day, Michael eating mayonnaise and black olives because he didn't have any ice cream, Andy taping his nipples so they didn't chafe during the Fun Run, and the greatest scene of all (during our all-time favorite episode, "Stress Relief: Part 1"): Dwight cutting the face off the mannequin during CPR training to pretend he was Dr. Hannibal Lecter.

While watching together, the delay was also amusing. Leslie would laugh at a joke two seconds before I heard it on my TV and chuckled. It sounded like I was slow on the uptake. …*Oh, I get it! Good one.*

We watched the Oscars and the Grammys together, too. I couldn't find the speaker on my TracFone, so I had to hold the phone up to my ear for three or four straight hours. I switched hands throughout the awards shows, yet by the time the final winners were announced, both arms were numb and I wanted to throw the phone through the TV.

When Leslie visited, she found the speaker on my phone in less than ten seconds.

I wasn't nearly as good of a tour guide as she'd been when I visited Memphis. I couldn't take her to the zoo or to the Stockyards because of her strong feelings about caging animals. She even hated it when we came across a horse-drawn carriage. She wanted to yank the driver down and set the horse free from dragging around an oversized load in suffocating humidity and chaotic traffic. I had to admit, it was a fair point I hadn't considered.

I couldn't take her to Angelo's, which served the best chopped beef sandwich in the world, because she was a vegan. I couldn't take her to play tennis with Todd and Bryan or to jam with the band because that didn't make for a romantic, secluded weekend. We couldn't play basketball, hit in the batting cages, or attend a Rangers game because, frankly, she wasn't a dude. I began realizing how many "guy" things I did on a regular basis.

What I could do was introduce her to Bryan and his parents. They'd been eager to meet her, so we chitchatted for a bit in their living room as Bryan played host, dutifully fetching refreshments for everyone. Leslie and Bryan connected right away, for which I was grateful. Bryan was like a power drill that arrived in the mail fully charged ready to go. He overwhelmed some people, and in fact, he told me many times how he'd burned out most of his previous friends and I was one of the only ones still standing. I was nervous he'd be too much for Leslie to handle, leaving me in an awkward conundrum, yet they joked and got on like they were old friends.

Leslie and I continued our tradition of playing putt-putt each visit. My goal was to shoot a thirty-six, par for the course. Maybe next time. We went to the Kimbell Art Museum and each picked our favorite painting, another tradition that had begun at the Dixon Gallery and Gardens in Memphis. We walked through the Botanic Garden and around the seminary campus where Bryan toiled and I'd survived.

I didn't take her to meet Richard and Della because there was only so much we could do in two days and she was already bordering on overload. It was supposed to be a relaxing weekend for us to spend time together alone, not meet everyone in town. Richard and Della would have to wait till next visit, which they completely understood.

I'd intentionally made sure our band didn't have any gigs that weekend so I'd be free for Leslie, though in hindsight, that was probably a mistake. She even asked, "When do I get to see you perform?"

"Uh...we're opening for Coldplay on their next tour," I answered, a bit caught off-guard. "Clear next summer."

"I want to see you stage dive," she teased.

"Then it's a good thing you have a medical background."

Playing on stage would've impressed her, I realized too late. *Rats*, I thought, kicking myself. Yet I still could play my guitar for her, which I did in her hotel room one evening. I played her a new song for which I'd written the music and Manya had penned the lyrics. I didn't try to sing the lyrics—I couldn't remember them all, anyway. Manya had titled it "Hummingbird," which I liked, and it was while I played this song that I later learned Leslie fell in love with me. She said it was the way the song changed tempos and even time signatures that reminded her of how I interacted with her: patient and sensitive, then zany and humorous, and back. She said it was my willingness to bend to the shape she needed that showed her my true character and thoughtfulness.

Of course, she didn't tell me that until later. When I finished playing, she got mad at me for something I couldn't quite comprehend and in just a few short minutes, we were on the brink of breaking up. Again, it wasn't until later that she confessed her realization of her feelings for me spooked her so much she pushed me away as hard as she could. This was scary territory rife with intimacy, full disclosure, and long-term commitment. That was a lot to absorb in one song. So Leslie picked a fight to elude the truth like she was a running back chased by an entire defense. She had to outrun it before being pinned under a massive dog pile with no way to squirm out and no room to breathe. She hoped I'd take the bait and fight back so vehemently the end would be unavoidable. I could let her off the hook before it was too late. I was the cause of this, and the solution.

But I didn't. It would've been easy enough to let happen. I struggled with emotional accessibility, verbalizing feelings, acceptance of love, assumptions of inadequacy—even *hugging.* I was more terrified than she in this minefield. We both could've let each other off the hook in one fight. Yet, in the end, I didn't want her to leave. I wasn't ready for it to end. I liked having someone who listened as if what I was saying were the most important thing she'd heard all day, because it was. This was a new one on me. It was hard to let go of something so rare I probably wouldn't find again. Mattering to that degree was as singular as it got.

CHAPTER FIFTEEN

Something Important

It was a blessing in disguise. I'd known for a while that Bryan needed to leave the band. As much as it fueled his motivation and buoyed his spirits, learning new parts, rehearsing, and playing shows took way too much time away from his studies. He wasn't the type of person who could multitask as effectively as if he focused on one main objective. Neither was I. He needed to pare down his outside interests and zero in on school from here out. He was already studying hard and had come a long way, but in the fall, he was up for practicum again. This was his time to put the pedal down for the finish line. He could impress people, make key connections, sharpen his craft, and begin building a bridge to a career. Figuring out a new guitar part at 11:30 at night didn't fit in with that.

Unfortunately, however logical the bottom line, it didn't make signing it any easier when it involved surrendering a dream.

I didn't have the nerve to bring it up. I was certain he'd misinterpret it as an indictment of his musicianship, that he was holding back the band and we were better off without him. In reality, it would've done him a favor. Our band wasn't going to make it, and any further time he invested in it would be wasted. I wanted him to be successful in counseling. He had a heart for helping people, especially kids, and he was a good listener. I could see him excelling in the field. I wanted him to give it his best shot. Yet I was terrified broaching the subject would send him into an emotional tailspin.

Thankfully, Manya did it for me. I'd never spoken to her about it, but she pulled me aside one day and said she wanted to alter our musical direction, incorporate a cellist, maybe a French horn, and let Bryan focus on school. She, too, recognized the crossroads where he stood, though she understood far better than I that we needed to make this choice for him. He wasn't ready to desert us, as he would've viewed it, and he still believed he could carry the surplus without anything slipping. He had to be told, not asked, and it had to be her because I couldn't do it.

The next day, she talked to Bryan and it was done. Simple as that. I braced for the fallout, yet it never came. He seemed mildly disappointed but in a way relieved. Even he had to admit that not driving an hour and a half round trip to Dallas three times a week was only going to make his life easier. I said, "Won't be the same without you." Then I extended an offer I hadn't planned on making but felt like the right thing to do: "Listen, if it's too weird with me still in the band, I'll drop out. No big deal."

He shook his head, and said, "No way, I'm fine. Go for it. Seriously."

That was when I knew he'd turned the corner. The old Bryan from just a year ago would've locked his bedroom door for days after getting booted from the band, like after his practicum denial. He would've let everything slide and given up. Yet this 2.0 version could handle a little adversity, a letdown here and there, without crashing into a tree. He smiled, and said, "Don't worry, I've always got the One Thing method to fall back on if things get hard."

The One Thing method was a trick I'd told him a while back to help push through a trying day. He just had to pick one thing to look forward to that evening, whether it was a movie or his favorite TV show or a chocolate malt from Fuddruckers. Something fun he enjoyed that he could focus on instead of the anxieties and depressing thoughts vying for his attention. It was pretty simplistic, yet it had helped him, which was enough.

So I soldiered on in the band without him. It felt odd driving back from Dallas late at night without Bryan studying next to me wearing a cap with his flashlight taped on, his school books stacked on the dashboard in front of him and on the floorboards, empty bags of sunflower seeds on the center console. More than odd, a little hollow. We'd started this together, yet I'd left him on the side of the road and driven off. The car and the purpose now seemed empty.

But it wouldn't be long before I joined Bryan, my days as a musician numbered, too. The number and fashion didn't line up with the picture I imagined, though I'd grown used to that.

Richard was striking out in the dog department. He'd found a trainer in Tennessee who prepared a service dog for him. When it was time to pick up the dog, Richard, Della, and I drove to Tennessee to meet Richard's new sidekick. It was fun being on the road with them. Richard was like an excited little kid going to meet Santa, while Della remained positive and optimistic no matter what we encountered. In the middle of a traffic jam, I grumbled, "Looks like we'll be here a while."

She immediately replied, "Perfect. Let's play 'I Spy' or count how many different license plates we can find." It took a whole heap of trouble to bring her down.

At the training facility, our party fizzled. The dog wouldn't, or couldn't, respond to Richard's commands. The trainer hadn't been able to simulate his slurred speech, so the dog wasn't used to hearing his name or "Sit" the way Richard pronounced it. The dog simply stared at Richard like he was speaking Cantonese.

On top of this, while Richard tried to direct the dog, his trainer kept admitting, "Oh, we should've worked on that," or "Yeah, that would've been good to practice." What the heck had they been doing out here for the last few months, playing backgammon? We'd driven all the way to Tennessee for this?

Richard decided to leave the dog with the trainer for additional work, though on the drive home he conceded the dog probably wasn't the one. Too much retraining, rewiring, starting over from scratch.

Troy was proving a tough act to follow. More like impossible.

Naturally, this was a blow to Richard's morale, yet ever Mr. Persistent, he stayed the course and continued seeking alternate avenues through which to secure a new service dog. He was determined to have that bond again. It had worked in the past with his other service dogs, and it could work again. He just had to find the right one.

Admirably, he didn't allow the disappointment to affect his schoolwork, as he remained on schedule to graduate with his master's degree the following year. He studied hard, and Della told me she'd found him numerous times camped in front of his computer late at night struggling to stay awake so he could complete his assigned reading.

As with Bryan, I wanted Richard to succeed. He'd overcome a lot and logged many hours of diligent work that others didn't have to. It took him twice as long to read a chapter, take a test, and write a paper. Like Bryan, he struggled with ADHD, as well as fatigue, sleep apnea, and memory and comprehension challenges that required rereading. And also like Bryan, he battled depression.

Despite the eternally optimistic glasses through which he viewed the world, Richard wasn't immune to moodiness and melancholy. Given his situation, it made perfect sense to me. I would've sulked all day unwilling to participate in life. Richard refused to play the victim card, yet he still fought off feeling sorry for himself. He just rarely talked about it. He didn't want to dump his gripes on everyone else because he already asked so much of them. Wasn't it enough they bathed him and brushed his teeth, fed and clothed him? Now they had to listen to him complain the whole time, too? He knew it wasn't fair, that he wouldn't have wanted to hear it if he'd been in their shoes, so he kept his sadness to himself most of the time.

Yet it was there, lurking, waiting for a vulnerable moment to crawl on top of his head and push him under. Such a moment had come years before I knew him, when he nearly succumbed to the hardships of life with cerebral palsy. It was after his divorce and his kids left to live with relatives, before Michael came back to stay with him. He was alone and despondent and saw no point in continuing. The deck was stacked against him and he was losing at life. He simply couldn't poke his head above the rising tide any longer. He was exhausted, with no one around to prove anything to except himself, and that simply wasn't enough anymore. At some point, moral victories and fighting the good fight felt as empty as his home, so he left one night to escape the reminders of what was missing and of what he'd missed out on.

He went to a lake to drown himself.

It was quiet with no one around, and he didn't hesitate. Once Richard made up his mind to do something, there was no turning back. He drove his chair straight to the edge of the water, but his wheels got stuck in the mud. Determined as ever, he slid down his chair into the mud to reach the water however he could. It didn't need to look pretty or go according to plan. Nothing else did, so why should this? He'd learned to be adaptable out of necessity. All that mattered was getting under the water.

He tried to drag himself into the lake, yet his left foot was stuck awkwardly in the mud and he couldn't free it. He struggled for twenty or thirty minutes to get out of the mud and into the water to finish what he'd started, but he couldn't make it. He finally put his head on the seat of his chair and cried, unable to control even his own death. He was powerless and useless and understood nothing.

Finally, he saw someone and called for help. He didn't want to, but what else was he going to do? Sit in the mud until morning? He didn't want anyone else calling an ambulance and then the paramedics carting him off to a psych ward when they discovered his suicidal intent. He asked the guy to come help, though he ended up calling EMT. However, when they arrived, EMT assumed Richard had merely gotten stuck and couldn't get out. He didn't tell them his real purpose, so they had no reason to send him to psychiatric care. They made sure he was okay, put him back in his chair, and sent him on his way.

Eventually, through counseling, time, prayer, Bible study, and Michael returning, Richard regained his footing. He got plugged into a church, gained a few friends and accountability partners, and worked his way back to the point when I'd met him, strong and resilient once again, bent but not busted.

Now, when things didn't work out, such as not finding a new service dog, Richard was able to weather the blow without buckling. He grieved and then regrouped. He snapped back undaunted.

To help ease the sting of this latest service dog not panning out, one of Richard's dreams came true. He'd always wanted a nice van in which he could sit up front in the co-pilot's spot. Now he had one. An old friend and mentor loaned him the money to buy a used Dodge Caravan without many miles on it. The van was red (I said goodbye to Big Blue and called this one Magnum after the red Ferrari 308 GTS used in *Magnum, P.I.*) and featured a ramp instead of a lift (no more accidental launches into orbit) and an EZ Lock Wheelchair Docking System on the floorboards into which Richard could secure his chair (no more lashing down the inmate). It was everything he'd ever wanted. It even had two working cup holders.

The best part was Richard could now get into the van and be ready to depart all by himself. He had a remote control on his key that opened the sliding door and lowered the ramp, and once inside the van, he could guide his chair into the EZ Lock without assistance. It was one more invaluable piece of independence he'd gained. Plus, he could now sit next to Della when they went places together, not behind her like she was his chauffeur. The van literally made his month, maybe his year.

The generosity of Richard's friend floored me, though Richard had every intention of paying him back. He began setting aside a little money each month toward the debt, slowly chipping away it like every other challenge before him. Hacking away at them all, piece by piece, piece by piece. I thought I was diligent before I met Richard, that I knew about perseverance, yet I was a beginner compared to him. I merely used diligence; he defined it. His survival depended on it. It wasn't a character trait he was building. It was an extension of his physical features, each fumbled item, slurred word, and drop of drool a war of will without respite. And he did it all with a smile like he'd been done a favor. At the time, I didn't understand that he had.

The next time I visited Leslie in Memphis, we attended Sunset Symphony. It was part of the annual Memphis in May International Festival that included the World Championship Barbecue Cooking Contest, the Beale Street Music Festival, and lots of artists, merchants, and food vendors everywhere. Leslie's favorite part was Sunset Symphony, held on the banks of the Mississippi River to close the monthlong festival. There was an air show with pilots buzzing low along the river, the Memphis Symphony Orchestra performing classic patriotic songs, a different legendary musical act headlining each year (we got to sing along with KC and the Sunshine Band – "Do a little dance…"), and of course, a staggering fireworks show to close the event that was the highlight for Leslie and for most spectators.

Growing up, I'd watched a few Fourth of July fireworks shows in D.C. from our church's roof a few blocks from the Capitol Building, and I'd never seen any better. But watching these enormous fireworks light up the night sky over the Mississippi River just might've topped them all. Leslie could've stood there for hours staring up at the colorful explosions peppering the black sky. She was a fiend for fireworks. We held hands, as I imagined telling her something important that would irrevocably change things between us. But was I sure? How did I know for *certain*? This type of statement couldn't be blurted without being positive, for there was no going back after it. When was the moment I knew? I later learned when she knew—she had the moment logged to the second when I played her "Hummingbird." But what about me?

Was it when she sent me a mock list of dating rules when we decided to "go steady," as they said back in the days of her favorite decade, the 1950s? One of the rules was I had to continue writing her hilarious letters that made her laugh out loud at least twice regardless of how long or often we spoke on the phone. Was it the first time I made her laugh so hard she snorted (a family trait her sisters and mom shared)? Was it when she read the last book I'd written in one sitting because she loved it so much? Was it the first time I called her Lucy because she reminded me of the Peanuts character? Was it one night when we were walking near her house and she stopped to talk to a homeless man for ten minutes and offered to bring him back a blanket and some clean clothes (which we later did)? Was it seeing how much love and respect she had for her mom, who reminded me in many ways of my mom? Was it the first time we held hands and I felt safe to let my guard all the way down?

Or was it a little of all these moments and more, rolled into one mound of certainty growing wider and more powerful as it bowled downhill like a runaway snowball?

It was definitely a mixture, yet if I had to pinpoint one moment, one event when I knew for sure, it was before I visited her for the first time. We were talking on the phone and I admitted to her that when I got nervous or hot or embarrassed, my face flushed red. I was very self-conscious about it and had never talked about it with anyone other than Mom. She responded with this: "Don't worry, it happens to me, too. We'll be the cutest little rosy-cheeked couple walking down the sidewalk." That was it. I knew I could be myself around her and that I could tell her anything without it being mocked or held against me in some way. There was trust, and where there was trust there could be intimacy, and love.

So now I knew, just as she did, yet neither of us was willing to let go of home base and march out into the middle all alone, exposed, with no way to take it back if it was too soon or too overwhelming for the other to hear. It was a gigantic step full of rippling ramifications, like tipping over the first of a thousand dominoes.

Though deep down I understood that first domino had been pushed the moment I began writing her.

The next day before I left for Texas, I told Leslie. She'd often asked what I was thinking whenever I looked in her eyes without saying anything. She liked to joke, "Are you picking which way you're going to kill me?" I'd smile and answer, "Just looking." But this time when she asked, I told her the truth.

She didn't say anything for a few moments. These were some long seconds of silence. Many thoughts flew through my head, none of them positive. *I should've waited. Too soon, too soon! Nice going, bud—just scared her off. I'm like human bug repellant. Why do I speak? Why do I open my mouth? Nothing good comes from talking. From now on, I'm telling everyone I'm mute.*

Then Leslie began crying, and the first thought I had was, *This was definitely not the right time to tell her.*

But then she said, "I never thought this would happen to me." Between sniffles, she told me she'd already said it to me dozens of times on the phone, just with the mute button pushed. Any time I made her laugh, or said something encouraging or thoughtful, she pressed the button to tell me. I had no idea, though that was the point. She added that each time she'd told me she adored me, that was code for loved, and she was sick of substituting words. "It's hard in the moment," she admitted. "I kept worrying I'd slip and say the wrong thing or forget to mute the phone."

It all felt surreal, but it was happening and the dominoes were tumbling full speed now. I knew what was next, what *had* to follow. We had to take a trip together. But not to the beach or to go camping. We had to fly to Boston and then rent a car to drive for an hour and a half to South Dennis on Cape Cod, where my folks lived. It was time for Leslie to meet Mom.

CHAPTER SIXTEEN

The South Shall Rise and Hug

Manya and I rehearsed with a drummer, bassist, and cellist, played a few shows, and even recorded a two-song demo. We added some new songs, shelved old ones, and eventually landed a headlining gig at a Dallas club where we'd opened once or twice for other bands. This was our time to shine. It was a relatively big step with the opportunity to win new fans and possibly gain more headlining shows. I hoped a local manager would see us and be so impressed he or she would take us on.

We actually had our best turnout for any show. Singers and musicians from other bands attended. It felt significant, and we tried to make the most of the moment. Unfortunately, after forty-five minutes, we were done. We'd been allotted another hour to play as the headliner, yet we ran out of songs. We'd discarded so many older songs to make room for new material, we had enough prepared for only one set. But we weren't in one-set territory anymore. This was two-hour, carry-the-evening, everybody-wanted-to-hear-more terrain. Not, "That's all we've got, thanks for coming out." Even if some of the older songs weren't quite as good as newer ones, it still would've been better to play them than nothing. By that point in the show, most of the crowd was somewhat inebriated and simply wanted to hear loud, live music. They weren't picky; they just didn't want it to be over.

As I packed up my gear, sweating profusely in front of everyone, it felt different than before, like something had changed during the course of this one performance. I was frustrated and tired with a long drive ahead of me, but it was more than that. Somehow I knew this was our last show.

It was a combination of factors: Bryan's absence left it a little less fun and fulfilling (he was the only reason I'd started writing songs in the first place); I wished we kept older tunes in our arsenal; I needed to move to Dallas, but I couldn't and didn't really want to; and I still struggled to connect the dots in my head as to how we could journey from Manya's garage to a successful touring act. All of that, coupled with the major time investment for driving and practicing, left me ready to quit.

Yet Manya's voice was so special, I had a hard time letting go. I knew this wouldn't happen again. Thankfully, Manya did the heavy lifting for me, as she did with Bryan. She knew it was time for us to try new things, that our band had run its course. She told me she wanted to pursue being a solo artist, allowing her the chance to write and perform her own songs exclusively, which made sense to me. My favorite part about being a musician was writing songs, so it was stifling for a singer like Manya to be limited in her writing opportunities because of other members in the band. I was surprised she'd lasted this long learning our songs. I agreed it was a good point to call it a day, and we set up a time for me to drive over to collect the cables and gear I stored in her garage.

That Saturday, I drove to her house to get my equipment. While alone in her garage, I stopped packing for a moment and looked around imagining the years we'd spent in here shivering in the cold or sweating in the heat while hashing out new songs. I remembered the frozen pizzas she always had ready for Bryan and me, and how her daughter liked to sing along when we practiced. I thought about the times we all went to shoot pool and play tennis and how nervous we'd been when we'd first met. My thoughts traveled even further back to when Bryan and I began playing music together in the living room of the apartment where Tripp and I lived near the seminary. I borrowed Tripp's twelve-string acoustic guitar to learn how to play, yet I broke a string about once a week from strumming too hard. I quickly memorized the route to the music store. I recorded a shoebox full of cassette tapes with new songs, mostly a cappella as I learned to play guitar and piano, and mostly bad. Yet there were a few that worked that we ended up keeping, and the feeling of creating a little piece of music that touched people sank its hooks deeply in me. Now, it was by far the hardest part to lose.

I said goodbye to Manya and wished her good luck, sincerely encouraging her to push forward with her music. Her talent was too unique to keep to herself. I loaded my gear in my car and drove back to Fort Worth. On the way, I couldn't help but wonder if all of this had been wasted time—not just here in Dallas, but even back to our first band in Atlanta. Were the last fifteen years a mistake? Had I been blinded by my silly dream of sitting by a hotel pool late at night while on a world tour? Should I have ditched it to pursue a traditional career that would've come in quite handy now that Leslie and I were headed in a serious direction? I could've latched on at a newspaper or magazine somewhere, slowly worked my way up until I became a columnist. But that type of position wasn't offered overnight, and the years it took to earn one weren't available to me anymore. The window had closed, and all I had to show for chasing my dreams was a few boxes of cables and an old mic stand with duct tape wrapped around its cracked base.

I glanced at one of the boxes dumped in Bryan's seat. He'd been working on a paper at home when I left. The fact that he could diligently plug away on schoolwork without me monitoring him was a huge leap forward. He'd come a long way from the days of me worrying he might kill himself if his depression grew too intense. I'd played a role in helping him, though several others had contributed significantly, and of course, Bryan had done the hardest part. Maybe that was what all these years of music were about. The songs and bands and gigs and endless practicing were really about helping Bryan, about putting someone else's needs first, like with Richard. Not about record deals and hits but friendship, loyalty, and personal growth. As it said in the book of Proverbs, "A friend loves at all times, and a brother is born for adversity." Bryan was like a brother to me, and the journey to help him reach this point was worth the years.

Plus, Bryan had always been a big fan of my writing and encouraged me to keep at it. Without his support, I might've scrapped it somewhere along the way. I was beginning to understand that success wasn't crossing a finish line first; it was not finishing alone. And these people I felt so proud to have helped overcome obstacles had probably pushed me just as hard.

Richard was kind enough to give me ten days off so I could take Leslie to Cape Cod to meet my parents. It was one of the many aspects of my job I'd come to love: my boss's flexibility. If I needed to go to the dentist or to pick up Bryan or to take Leslie to meet my folks, Richard was always agreeable. Every now and then, he tossed in a tiny guilt trip like, "Well, if you really have to go…" But that was understandable and was as loud as his protests rose. He was considerate and generous, and I doubted another boss would've been as accommodating.

I'd grown up going to Cape Cod. My grandfather owned a house in South Dennis that had been passed down in our family for generations, and we took our annual two-week vacation there each August. When my grandfather died, he left the house to my mom. A few years later, my parents finally sold their home in Maryland and moved to the Cape.

The house on the Cape had four bedrooms and one bathroom, which wasn't convenient in the mornings or before bed when my whole family visited, yet we were used to it since our house in Maryland had only one full bathroom (there was a half bathroom in my dad's workshop downstairs he practically boarded up to keep us from using to limit traffic through his maze of tools). The Cape house also had a parlor, workshop, and garage, and when my folks moved in, they renovated the kitchen and bathroom and had a porch built. Dad also constructed a shed out back (to go along with the other shed next to it) to house all of his tools. Within just a few years, both sheds, the workshop, the loft above the workshop, the garage, and even Mom's new porch were all filled to capacity with Dad's lathe, milling machine, band saw, and every other tool he'd stockpiled over the decades. They had their own coastal hardware store.

During our visits to the Cape when my three older brothers and I were growing up, we never toured the peninsula. In fact, we rarely strayed outside of Dennis. We weren't big sightseers. We kept the same basic routine for years on our vacations: played baseball in the yard, read, walked down to Bass River a few minutes away, piled in the car at three to drive to West Dennis Beach (the nearest beach), and possibly ate fish for dinner if Andy caught any (in later years, he liked to fish on charter boats). We played putt-putt once a trip, took a ride on my grandfather's old boat, and finished the vacation with dessert at Friendly's. That was it. Nothing too exciting, but it was nice being near the water in less humidity, with a big yard in which to play.

Things changed when I took Leslie to the Cape. For the first time, I rented a car and we explored different towns outside of Dennis. I joked with Leslie, "I wonder if we'll have to show our IDs at the border." This was foreign territory for me, branching out beyond the familiar, comforting boundaries of Dennis. We visited Chatham, Harwich, Orleans and even went up to the Outer Cape for a day in Provincetown. It was another world right next door I'd never seen. It reminded me of growing up in Oxon Hill, Maryland, near the D.C. line. We never once traveled to Baltimore to see an Orioles game, though they played in the same state. Baltimore was an hour away yet felt like the other side of the country. Truro, Wellfleet, and Provincetown were forty minutes to an hour away from South Dennis but might as well have been on another continent when we were growing up.

Provincetown was our favorite spot Leslie and I explored. We loved the art galleries, bookstores, antique shops, clothing markets, and every kind of restaurant imaginable, all lined up on Commercial Street right by the Atlantic Ocean. It looked like something out of a movie. They loved dogs here, too, which appealed to us. Many of the storeowners even left out bowls of water for the pooches. Leslie said, "We should've brought Bear, Dill, and Atti." They would've been warmly welcomed.

There was actually more to do in Provincetown than we could squeeze into one visit, with whale watching, dune tours, and several galleries on the to-do list for next time. We were definitely coming back. I felt like I was finally learning a little about Cape Cod after visiting my whole life. There was a lot more here than just putt-putt and Friendly's, though Leslie and I did continue our tradition of playing a round of miniature golf (still no thirty-six for me, or Leslie).

Mom liked Leslie right away. They'd already had good conversations on the phone, yet I was nervous for them to meet in person, especially with Dad interjecting every chance he got. He had a way of dominating the room and the house. I worried Mom and Leslie wouldn't get much time alone, or it would be rushed and guarded.

My fears were unwarranted, because both Mom and Dad treated Leslie like a Southern belle just up from the plantation. Mom had long carried a fascination with the Civil War and the South—her favorite book was *Gone with the Wind.* While I lived in Atlanta, Mom had mentioned more than a few times that the classic novel's author, Margaret Mitchell, was buried there. She couldn't understand why I hadn't visited her grave at Oakland Cemetery. She even looked up directions.

Mom and Dad swooned over Leslie's accent, turning each of her words into a leisurely stroll down a tree-lined, country lane. I really didn't have to do much except sit back and let Leslie speak. It was much easier than I'd anticipated. At one point, I even got up to get a drink in the kitchen, leaving the three of them in the living room, when I spotted an interesting magazine. About half an hour later, Mom and Leslie came out to the kitchen to find me sitting at the table engrossed in an article. I got a good death glare from Leslie over leaving her alone with my parents after they'd just met. *Sorry,* I mouthed sheepishly.

Mom gave Leslie a tour of the house, minus the tool sheds and garage. Dad showed her those later, though it was difficult for more than one person at a time to wiggle in. As Mom and Leslie walked down the hall to the stairs to see the second floor, Leslie noticed an antique tea set in a cabinet to her left. She commented how beautiful it was. Mom later told me that no one had ever mentioned anything about her tea set, and that if Leslie and I married one day, she'd give it to her.

A southern accent *and* liking Mom's tea set—Leslie was batting a thousand.

Leslie looked through our old family photo albums, teasing me about the colorful, plaid outfits my brothers and I used to wear. They practically glowed. Mom must've found a sale one weekend.

Dad hovered nearby, almost treating Leslie like a new tool he'd just bought. He was quite excited to have her here with them. Multiple times throughout the day, he knocked on the door to the parlor where she stayed (one of only three rooms besides my parents' bedroom and the kitchen with a window air conditioning unit) to see if she needed anything. He seemed concerned she might run away.

We ate every dinner at the dining room table, which was reserved for Thanksgiving and extremely special occasions. Mom even used the fancy tablecloth. I felt like I should slip on a suit coat. When it was just Mom and Dad here, they ate dinner in the living room in front of the evening news. Back when I was fourteen and Andy and David had both moved out of our house in Maryland, dinners in our tiny sauna of a kitchen stopped for good. Suddenly, we were free to eat wherever we wanted, so, naturally, Gordon, my third-oldest brother, and I headed for the TV. Mom and Dad soon followed and continued the practice on the Cape.

Emma, the beagle Mom and Dad had obtained from a rescue shelter a few years ago, snuggled up to Leslie's leg hoping to coax a treat or two off her plate. Emma knew a dog lover when she saw one. To Mom, this was another star in Leslie's crown. Mom was a super softy for dogs and had taken in ten over the years. We used to wake up with dogs sprawled across our legs. So the fact that Leslie had rescued five of her own (along with five cats), plus taken a shine to Emma, sealed the deal. Mom approved, though she'd already fallen in love with her on the phone. Dad was in, too, happy to have a fresh pair of ears to hear his endless stories.

The entire visit went as well as I could've hoped, except for our final morning. Leslie and I said goodbye to my parents but then got into a huge argument because I hadn't hugged Mom. This was a big deal to Leslie. Her family hugged and said they loved each other every day, so it was extremely unusual and unacceptable that my family didn't do this. Or, at least, that *I* didn't do it. The rest of my family wasn't her responsibility, but she wasn't going to let me get away with it anymore. I tried to explain this was how we'd always interacted, that it would've been awkward for all involved if I started hugging folks like we were at a wake. "I'd probably get punched," I told her.

"You'll get used to it," she replied matter-of-factly.

"Not every family's like yours," I insisted.

"No, but you can hug your mama. It's not that big of a sacrifice. And she'll probably appreciate it a lot more than you think."

We ended up driving back to my parents' house so I could hug Mom. She opened the front door and met me on the step. "Is everything all right?" she asked.

I glanced over my shoulder at Leslie, who somehow managed to smile and wave at Mom while drilling holes through my skull with her eyes. She was talented.

I'd hugged Mom before, yet admittedly it had been a long time. In a family with five guys, it simply wasn't on our radar much. We didn't even shake hands or high-five each other on the basketball court. Actually, we didn't say hello that often. Nodding was our preferred mode of communication.

Mom stared at me, waiting for an answer. I finally shrugged and said, "Don't freak out," and leaned over and hugged her. Then I whispered, "I love you, Mom."

She said, "Why, thank you, my dear. I love you, too." When we pulled apart, she was smiling and peeking over my shoulder like she knew exactly who was behind this. As I walked back to our rental car, I turned to see Mom waving her fist above her head to Leslie, who returned the fist wave. They had me surrounded.

When I got in, Leslie said, "See, that wasn't too painful, was it?"

I saw the wide grin on Mom's face as she stood on the step waving to us, and I answered, "No, not too bad."

CHAPTER SEVENTEEN

A Part to Play

That fall, Bryan's moment of truth arrived. He applied for his practicum a second time, knowing if he didn't get accepted, his future would look much bleaker. I was ready to camp outside the homes of whichever administrators and professors were making the decision, holding up signs reading, "FREE BRYAN," "EQUALITY FOR ALL," and maybe even, "LET MY PEOPLE GO." Backup sign ideas included, "HE WON'T KILL ANYONE" and "I'VE GOT A GRENADE."

I also considered bribes and blackmail, though I didn't possess any incriminating evidence to dangle over someone's head, and I only had enough money to bribe them with lunch at Subway. Regretfully, I had to forgo these options.

Bryan handled the wait much calmer than I. My focus was solely on the negative consequences of him getting rejected, how bad the meltdown would be, how far the free fall. I didn't even bring up practicum for fear it would launch him into a state of panic, though maybe that was more for my benefit. Bryan seemed unrattled by the whole process, even confident. Maybe a little too confident. He mentioned one morning, "I'm looking forward to actually working with clients and not just reading about it."

I contemplated revisiting the extortion route.

He'd come so far and made such progress, I didn't want to see him suffer another setback. I wondered if there was a certain number of failures each person could withstand before apathy automatically kicked in, like we were on the clock from birth in a race against ourselves. If that were true, the seconds had to be ticking down on Bryan.

Yet another possibility Richard and Bryan were opening my eyes to was that, from the right perspective and with a positive attitude, setbacks increased strength, fortitude, and drive. They could be fed upon as fuel to push forward until breaking through. It was hard to believe, but maybe failure was actually a good thing, at least in doses. As we waited for the news, I sincerely hoped so.

The only time Bryan appeared nervous was the day the letter arrived. He sat on the end of his bed and handed it to me. "You read it," he said, lowering his head. As I took a deep breath and carefully opened the envelope like it was plutonium, I briefly considered lying if it was disaster, though I couldn't think of a plausible substitute. *Hey, guess what? They're really excited about letting you know their decision just as soon as time permits.* That made a lot of sense.

I had no choice but to read it verbatim. Why put off the inevitable? He'd find out one way or another. Better to hear it from me.

When I read the word "pleased" in the opening line, I exhaled. Bryan was in. He'd been officially accepted into practicum and would start this semester. "You did it, bud!" I exclaimed. "You're in. Way to go."

At first, he didn't say anything. He didn't even raise his head. I wasn't sure if he'd heard me, or believed me. Yet then without looking up, he lifted his fist above his head in celebration, a lot like Mom on the Cape. Everybody was doing it.

Bryan looked relieved, and I realized he'd been much more worried these last few weeks, even months, than he'd let on. He admitted, "I didn't know what I was going to do if I didn't get in. Maybe Mexico—I hear the cartels are hiring," he added with a grin.

"Why didn't you say anything?" I asked.

He stood up, answering, "No sense stressing you out more."

I smiled to discover that at some point during his many late nights studying while I slept, Bryan had quietly switched our seats to start looking out for me. He could take care of himself now. But much more, he'd grown strong and stable enough to protect others. He was more than on the right track—he was leading the way.

Della was one of the most selfless people I'd met. It was in her DNA to put others first. So when her daughters' homesickness persisted and the girls begged to move back to Tennessee, she swallowed hard and said goodbye to Evelyn and Emilee. She was now separated from all four of her kids, and I knew it was only a matter of time before the divide grew too great and she rejoined them. They were her babies—she couldn't be expected to live without them, at least not until they were grown. As much as she loved Richard, I seriously doubted she would've been willing to move to Texas if a few of her kids hadn't tagged along. Evelyn and Emilee had viewed it as an adventure, though it wasn't their idea. This was Della's journey, and the thrill of change had worn off for her kids. Della couldn't hold them against their will—she had to let them go. But it wouldn't be for long. I knew sometime soon Richard would have to make the same sacrifice as Della and leave home. What I didn't know was where that would put me, and when.

To accompany Della's bad news, Richard received some of his own. A trainer in Fort Worth had been diligently working with a German Shepherd puppy to take over as Richard's new service dog. Richard and the trainer both thought training a puppy before he had a chance to learn any other habits would solve bonding and communication issues. However, when Richard took possession of the dog, he and Della quickly learned that he had bladder problems. He was supposed to be housebroken yet clearly wasn't. After a while, Richard took him to the vet to discover the dog had more than typical puppy bladder struggles, but internal problems as well. When the issue persisted and wouldn't improve, Richard had no choice but to send the puppy back to the trainer until further notice.

Richard was heartbroken and didn't know what else to do. He'd spent so much time and energy trying to find a new service dog, yet something always went wrong to prevent it. He didn't understand why. He'd never encountered these types of obstacles with his other service dogs. Decades without any major problems. But now he couldn't catch a break, and he was starting to wonder if maybe God didn't want him to find a new service dog. Perhaps this was a sign that Richard needed to focus more on Della to strengthen their bond. With another service dog, his attention would be divided, and Della needed all of Richard right now with her kids gone.

After a few days of moping, he finally said to me, "Maybe I'm supposed to lay this down."

I tried to put a positive spin on it, and said, "Or maybe it's not the right time. You just got married not too long ago. That's a huge change. You're getting close to graduating. There's lots of big stuff in your life already. It might be better for you, and the dog, if you waited a little while so you can focus on it properly."

He thought about this for a few moments and said, "Yeah, maybe...maybe it's for the best. Maybe God's holding me back for a reason."

"He must be using both hands to hold you back."

He laughed and replied, "You know me—full speed ahead."

It was good timing for a break from dog hunting because Richard was finishing his last two classes to earn his master's degree in religion with a minor in pastoral counseling. It had been a long, tedious road, but his diligent hard work had paid off. I vividly recalled our last-minute, frantic scramble to pass his first class just under the wire. Our time management had improved, yet there were days when his degree track felt endless. All of the punishing hours listening to Computer Lady read textbooks as only she could. The constant papers, discussion boards, sermons, and projects. I'd begun dreading syllabus day at the beginning of each new session.

But as we crawled across the finish line to complete the second of our three major goals (marriage and master's down, job search ahead), the late hours and mountain of work were all worth it. He'd finished, and nobody anywhere could ever take it away. For the rest of his life, whenever Richard spoke at an elementary school or at a church (which he now had more time to do), he'd be introduced as having cerebral palsy *and* undergraduate and master's degrees. That was enough to stop anyone from jumping to inaccurate conclusions about the capabilities of people with disorders.

This called for a celebration, so we decided to throw Richard a graduation party at a local church. However, an intimate, low-key gathering wasn't what Richard had in mind. He had something bigger in store. He rented a freestanding lift and planned to use it to stand up during "Rise Again" by Dallas Holm to show that anything was possible through Christ and one day he'd stand in heaven. Unfortunately, his plan included two oversights: First, the song was about Jesus rising from the dead, not standing in heaven; second, and much more importantly, Richard never wore a belt or underwear, so as soon as he was fully upright, his pants would fall straight down, kicking off the real party.

None of us even thought about his lack of a belt until he was already strapped in about to attempt the feat. The light bulb flashed in my head and I jumped up from my table and raced over to the lift as a few of Richard's larger friends tried to wrestle him into position. Della hurried over, too, having figured out the crowd was about to witness a striptease. Both of us took turns whispering in Richard's ear about the belt blunder, yet while he acknowledged it was a problem, he still seemed optimistic he could pull it off if we found some rope to slide through his belt loops.

I looked at Della, amazed and frustrated by his determination, and shook my head. "Richard," I said, "we don't have any rope. This is a church, not Home Depot. I don't know, maybe they have rope somewhere, but it'd take too long to find. These people are waiting."

Della suggested, "Why don't you just tell them what this represents, what the song means to you? I think that'd still be very powerful."

We both waited for the verdict, as the big guys kept struggling to make the lift work with Richard. Thankfully, they couldn't, and Richard finally decided to abort the plan. It just wasn't safe—there was a good chance he would've fallen and hurt himself. Plus, there was the whole nudity aspect to consider.

When he was buckled back into his wheelchair, Richard took Della's suggestion and told everyone the point behind the lift demonstration. He also expressed his sincere gratitude for their love and support, not only while he'd worked on his degree, but for the entire time he'd known and leaned on them. He said, "I know I'm a pain in the butt," which got a good laugh, "but when you lift me up, I fly like an eagle."

This segued nicely to his next musical selection, Chris Tomlin's "I Will Rise," with its lyrics, "And I will rise when He calls my name, no more sorrow, no more pain. I will rise on eagles' wings, before my God fall on my knees." I thought this would've been a much better selection for the lift stunt, though maybe it would've been too overwhelming because as we all listened quietly to the song, Richard began sobbing so hard he had to drive his wheelchair to the other side of the giant curtain dividing the basketball court where we sat. For the remaining two and a half minutes of the song, everyone squirmed in their chairs listening to Tomlin sing and Richard wail as he drove slowly in circles down by the other basketball goal. It was awkward, yet we knew he was happy and thankful, so we let him be.

After the song ended, Richard regrouped and rejoined us. As I watched him chat with a few friends, I thought about the fact that, although he was pushing fifty years old, he'd remade his life. He'd gone back to school, remarried, and graduated. He was living proof that it was never too late to start over, to change direction to a better course, and that everyone had something to offer. Most people, including me, felt they didn't have anything truly insightful to share with others, a significant, life-altering word to impart. But Richard showed me it was impossible to know who needed to hear exactly what only I could say, and that if withheld, that person lost out. I held the power to hurt someone just with my silence. It was a sobering thought. How many people had I met who could've used a little encouragement, or a simple piece of advice from my unique perspective that would've made a world of difference to them? How many friends had wanted to vent anxieties and fears yet needed me to inquire first? How many just wished I'd listen?

Everyone had something to offer because everyone else had a need. No one was exempt, and no excuse valid. There was no getting off the hook with this. We all played a part.

Through an extreme stroke of good luck, Leslie found an accidental posting online for a $30 room rate for the Joule, a five-star downtown hotel in Dallas. It should've read $300. Before they could realize their mistake, she quickly booked a three-night stay that included free valet, breakfast, and a massage. It was the steal of the year. The Joule had a world-class spa, an outdoor pool on the tenth floor that extended eight feet out from the building over Main Street (the pool had a plexiglass wall at the end so swimmers could see pedestrians, and vice versa), restaurants, retail boutiques, an art collection, and was close to the Dallas Arts District and less than a mile from Dealey Plaza (the JFK assassination fascinated me).

Of course, when Leslie visited, I drove over each day from Fort Worth to make a thorough inspection of the hotel to ensure her safety. Didn't want her to be at risk in the big city. I checked the pool several times.

We also attended an outstanding Weepies concert in Dallas

that weekend. They were one of our favorite bands. We toured the sixth floor of the Texas School Book Depository, now a museum, where Lee Harvey Oswald supposedly fired three shots in six to eight seconds to kill President Kennedy, though I had my doubts. In later years, accomplished marksmen using the identical model of Oswald's rifle couldn't load and fire three shots that fast, and certainly not that accurately. None of it made much sense, which only intrigued me more. Leslie probably got more enjoyment out of watching me scurry around the museum like a curious kid in a toy store than from the exhibits themselves.

We went to Neiman Marcus and other fancy shops and stores downtown, the Dallas Museum of Art, and Galleria Dallas. The weather was beautiful. It was a perfect weekend.

Except for one thing.

Leslie thought I was going to propose.

I didn't.

She didn't confess this until later, so at the time, I thought everything went great. She did seem a little distracted the day she left for Memphis. It turned out she wasn't distracted, she was using every ounce of strength she had not to burst into tears until her drive home. I'd ruined the weekend without even knowing it. On what was supposed to be a dream trip when she got engaged, I'd given her a hug and a kiss and told her to drive safely.

I didn't propose because I wasn't ready. It wasn't that I couldn't see spending my life with Leslie. It was that I knew the moment I asked, I'd let go of everything simple and safe for a challenge so terrifying it made working for Richard look like guarding an empty parking lot. I preferred predictability—I clung to it. If I'd lived in generations past, I would've been a riveter on an assembly line all day. Or better yet—an old-school file clerk back in the days of shelves stacked with paper in actual files. I could've hidden in those rows of boxes for years feeling quite content. Marrying Leslie was like strapping myself to a rocket to launch into space without a flight plan. I didn't have a career or savings or any answers. Nothing about it felt controllable. Worse, it seemed reckless, like I could inflict serious damage with one fateful question.

Still, I brooded over it on a weekly basis. It wasn't going away. It rarely left my thoughts for long. It was the logical next step in our relationship. But sometimes steps looked like leaps, and logic and truth appeared incompatible.

CHAPTER EIGHTEEN

The Greatness of Junk

Now that Richard had his master's degree, it was time for him to look for a job. Of our three goals, this was the one I feared most. But it was a selfish concern. I did worry he wouldn't find something and become depressed, yet that wasn't what preoccupied my thoughts for the last few months of his degree program. I worried he actually *would* land a job. It was an awful thing to think, but I didn't want him to find a position.

I liked my job the way it was, going to Richard's house, working with him one-on-one, spending the day running errands, writing his emails, and working on sermons or lessons with him. I appreciated the flexibility of our schedule, the variety, and the bond we'd forged. Every day was something different, and each undertaking an opportunity for us to tackle it together at our own pace. We joked around and laughed, ate lunch at Julie's with Amy, stopped in to visit some of his oldest friends around town. After years with him, I still didn't dread going to work, which wasn't what I'd expected, and perhaps the most essential ingredient of longevity. The day it stopped being enjoyable and turned into drudgery that I didn't want to endure, I'd start thinking about leaving.

My fear was that Richard would find a job that changed the dynamics of our relationship, limiting our interaction and flexibility, while adding to my responsibilities, and all of it in front of a crowd of customers or a staff of employees. That sounded embarrassing, frustrating, interminable, and like a completely different position than the one for which I'd signed on.

It also sounded completely selfish. This wasn't about me. None of it. This was Richard's life I was supposed to be aiding, not mine—his needs I was putting ahead of my own. He wanted a job, to be more actively involved in the community, to feel like he was contributing something vital. Everyone wanted to be indispensable, including him. He'd worked for years in school for the chance to work in public, and now it was time to give it a shot. My job was to support him the best I could in all his endeavors, and he needed my help to make this kind of huge transition. It was daunting for anyone entering the work force. For a man with cerebral palsy confined to a wheelchair, it was Everest.

A division of Goodwill ran a program that assisted people with physical challenges to find jobs. Richard went for interviews and vocational testing. He answered questions and performed assessment drills. He tried his best, and I was never prouder of him than while he was there, because he faced all of his anxieties and insecurities head on, determined to find a place where he could help. It would've been much easier to stay at home than to expose himself to judgment and scrutiny. The world didn't care what he had to overcome. There were customers to serve and deadlines to meet to keep their doors open. Whoever did this best typically got the jobs.

Richard scored poorly on his vocational test, and the administrators concluded that he'd require too much help at a normal position. Basically, they told him there wasn't a job for which he was suited.

I'd never felt so guilty in my life.

Secretly, I'd hoped for this outcome, yet seeing the crushed look on Richard's face as we left the testing center for the final time pounded it into my thick skull that I'd been dead wrong to wish this upon him. He didn't deserve it as his reward for years of diligent studying. He didn't need to be told his speech impairment would probably confuse people. He was well aware of that already. He didn't have to be reminded that he operated at a slower pace than everyone else. He'd been playing catch-up his whole life. What he needed was affirmation and encouragement, and if they weren't going to give it to him, I would.

"Richard, these kinds of tests don't prove a thing," I insisted as we drove home. "They don't know you. They don't see you out in public. You're a people person. That's a gift. That can't be read on a graph."

He looked over at me but then turned for the window again.

"The folks at that center just met you," I persisted. "It's always tricky at first for people to get used to your speech. It was for me, too. But after that, everybody loves being around you. Look at Amy and Jody, or John at the Healthcare Store, or your friends from church. You guys have a blast together."

He shrugged, and mumbled, "I guess."

"What about Della? You really think she would've fallen in love with you and moved all the way here to marry you if she didn't like talking to you? If she didn't enjoy your company? Politeness only goes so far."

I waited for his response, yet he didn't answer, so I gave it one more pass. "I guess what I'm trying to say is don't let them decide for you. Don't ever let anybody tell you what you can do. It's up to you. You're in charge."

He looked at me, unable to hide the smile poking out from underneath his scowl. He chuckled softly and said, "Who's the boss?"

"You are," I said, smiling, too.

"I'm the boss," he declared more emphatically while thrusting his right thumb at his chest.

"Preach it, Reverend."

"I'm in charge. I decide what I can do."

"Amen."

He paused and then said, "You know, you're starting to sound a lot like me. You're learning." Then he burst out laughing, followed by the obligatory coughing fit and drink from his cup.

To keep brightening his mood, I told him, "Oh, by the way, if you're still interested in meeting Leslie, she's coming to Fort Worth again." I knew he and Della were dying to meet her, but it hadn't worked out yet. Astoundingly, Leslie still wanted to come visit me, even after her massive letdown at the Joule. I was luckier than I realized. Richard announced, "She's coming for dinner, and that's final. I'll tell Della to start cooking," he added, giggling.

Two weeks later, Leslie and I were eating dinner in Richard and Della's kitchen. Della had prepared a delicious meal, which Richard and I devoured while the ladies got to know each other. Richard looked like the cat that ate the canary, bursting at the seams to ask something. Finally, he did. "So, when are you two getting married?" Subtle as always.

I almost dropped my fork. Leslie and I looked at each other, and all I could tell her was, "He says what's on his mind."

Della leaned toward Richard and playfully scolded, "You can't ask that. Don't put pressure on these two kids. They might leave without helping clean up."

I hoped our laughter would magically funnel us to a different topic, yet when the giggles subsided, the question still hung in the air like an elusive mosquito dodging the swatter. As awkward as Richard's inquiry had been, I could tell everyone at the table (especially Leslie) was interested in my answer, so I quickly told my boss in an attempt to diffuse the ticking bomb, "You'll be the first to know."

He smiled, and said, "I'd better."

Leslie corrected, "You can be the second to know, but I should probably be first."

I nodded, agreeing, "Sorry, Richard, she's got you there."

"I'm patient," he said. "But I'm second."

"*Richard,*" Della admonished.

I clapped my hands once, and said, "Okay, good, now that that's settled—Della, how's it going over there at the daycare center? You know, Leslie used to work as a nanny years ago." I smiled at Della, hoping she'd grab my clumsy baton handoff. She giggled like a little girl (I wasn't sure who had the cuter laugh, Leslie's snort or Della's little girl giggle) and answered, "Busy as ever. I had one baby the other day who threw up on me twice before I'd even had my morning coffee. Couldn't he have at least waited till after my coffee? How inconsiderate."

Leslie and I laughed, while Richard took a drink. We were now safely off the marriage topic. The mosquito had been nailed, and I could breathe again. Yet I knew it was merely borrowed time. I had to make a decision, and the longer I waited, the harder it would be. Big choices didn't grow easier upon further deliberation. It only provided more time to second-guess the decision that was probably made within the first two minutes the question appeared. I didn't need more weeks or months to figure out what to do. But knowing the answer didn't make the question any simpler.

Richard and I spent our time working on sermons and lessons he could give at local churches and elementary schools. He'd done this in the past, but now he wanted to do it much more frequently. He had a great testimony and much to share with young people, so I thought they could glean a lot from him.

After a few weeks of work, he spoke to the youth group at his own church, and then a week later he addressed the third-, fourth-, and fifth-graders at a nearby elementary school. At first, the kids were shy with him, overwhelmed by his slurred speech and unique physical appearance, but they quickly warmed up and asked all sorts of questions, some of them borderline inappropriate. Kids did say the darnedest things. One third-grader asked, "Do you pee in your pants?" Another fourth-grader asked, "Can you talk clearer, 'cause I can't understand you?" My favorite was from a fifth-grade boy who looked like he was fifteen (what were they feeding kids these days?), who asked, "Why don't you just go to the gym and, you know, do some squats? Get your legs stronger so you can walk." Richard looked over at me, as I wondered if perhaps the boy had tried fifth grade more than once.

Richard's next speaking engagement was at a fairly large church, where he was going to address the entire congregation for five to ten minutes during the morning service. It was a big opportunity, which he took seriously. He worked tirelessly on it, researching the passage from the Bible he planned to speak on and rewriting drafts. He even pushed back lunch at Julie's one day because he was on a roll and didn't want to lose his train of thought. His salad and sweet tea would have to wait!

He focused on the first three verses of the ninth chapter in the book of John. The passage read: "As He passed by, He saw a man blind from birth. And His disciples asked Him, 'Rabbi, who sinned, this man or his parents, that he would be born blind?' Jesus answered, 'It was neither that this man sinned, nor his parents; but it was so that the works of God might be displayed in him.'"

One morning as we worked, I said, "Do you mind if I ask you something?"

He swung his head over from the computer screen, answering, "Fire away."

I wasn't sure if it was completely appropriate, but we'd reached the point in our friendship where sensitive, personal areas were no longer restricted. We'd read the *Kama Sutra* together, for crying out loud. All boundaries vanished after that. I asked, "Is that how you feel? In the passage?"

"What do you mean?"

"Um..." I searched for the right words, unable to find a better approach than the direct one. "Your CP. Do you think that's why you were born with it? To show how God can use you, despite your physical challenge, to accomplish so much?"

Richard backed his wheelchair away from the table and turned to face me in my chair. When he had something important to say, he liked to point himself directly at the target. It reminded me of when he made me sit on the couch in the living room of his old house to confess that he was lonely and wanted to find a wife, which seemed like ten years ago. He said, "I'm glad God picked me to have cerebral palsy. You know why?"

I shook my head.

"Because it's hard. All the junk I've been through—it's good. It's great. It makes me lean on Him more." He stopped to think and then said, "Otherwise, who would I be? Just somebody without a care in the world. Nobody helping me. Don't have to ask for help. Don't have to be humbled. Just doing it all on my own." He motioned for his giant cup by the computer, so I gave him a quick drink. Then he asked, "Why were we created?"

I flashed back to my seminary education and answered, "To glorify God?"

He nodded and said, "Yeah, but even more than that, to have intimacy with Him. A relationship with the Creator. That's why He made us—to have fellowship with us." He moved his chair slightly closer to me and said, "When you were a kid, did you listen to your parents?"

I shrugged and replied, "Sometimes. Usually. But I was a wonderful boy," I added with a smile.

He laughed and said, "I bet. But when you were in trouble, did you ask them for help?"

"Sure."

"We don't talk to God unless we need help. We forget all about Him. We think we don't need Him. But that's not what He wants. He's our Father. He wants intimacy." He nodded and said, "My CP reminds me, and that's a blessing." He concluded by saying something I hoped I'd never forget as long as I lived, and I doubted I would: "I'm the luckiest man in the world."

For days afterward, I thought about what Richard said. I'd always viewed hardships and success from a completely opposite perspective. Struggles and failures were to be avoided at all costs, while success was sidestepping mistakes and oversights that prevented me from reaching goals. But was that the point of all this? To make my dreams come true? Smooth sailing down the Pacific Coast Highway?

Or was Richard right? Were the setbacks and stumbles the best part? When I was alone in my room ready to ditch it all, with nowhere else to turn but God, was that finally, ultimately, success? Was that the only way a sinner in a fallen world could stop obsessing over the surroundings for two seconds to see eternal significance? Maybe I did need crisis to rattle me out of cruise control. I had to be knocked down to look up.

I'd seen it incorrectly my whole life. Instead of raging over mistakes and wallowing in regret, I should've embraced them as opportunities to know God on a deeper level, to "lean not on my own understanding." To see the world from the proper perspective and to keep my priorities in check. This was the formula for true joy, the kind that didn't dilute in monotonous routine. It was the secret to enjoying life, and a man in a wheelchair with cerebral palsy who "wasn't suited" for a normal job had explained it to me. Finally. After years of groping in the dark for the light switch, Richard had flicked it on in between gulps from his Conoco cup. I was the blind one with the physical challenge from birth, not him. And he was the one taking care of me, tending to my needs, making sure I didn't have an accident. He was the one in charge, because he was the only one of us who understood he wasn't.

CHAPTER NINETEEN

Finding the Fishing Pier

I had a plan. To fool Leslie, I needed a good one because she could smell surprises a mile off. One Friday after work, I drove to Memphis to spend the night at her folks' house, and then in the morning I called Leslie pretending to still be in Fort Worth. She seemed a bit edgy and not in the greatest mood, but I refused to let us have an argument. Not on this day. No matter how grumpy she became, I was Mr. Rogers and spun it positively. "I'm sorry your head hurts, but I bet it feels better in just a few minutes!"

Then I had her mom call her to ask her to come out to their house that afternoon because she needed to talk to her about something. Naturally, this concerned Leslie, though her mom did an excellent job of not spilling the beans while assuring her nobody was dying of cancer and it could wait until the afternoon. I needed time to complete preparations.

Leslie's favorite spot in her parent's house was the deck on the third floor, so this was where it would go down. But first I had to get a few important things, like the ring. Her mom and I met Leslie's aunt (a jewelry expert) to find the perfect engagement ring, and we luckily spotted one we thought Leslie would love. I then went with her mom to pick out flowers, plus red roses to scatter petals across the deck.

Back at the house, I set out a chair on the deck, showered, put on my only suit, and waited until I saw Leslie's car turn up their long driveway before scattering the petals. I didn't want them all blowing away before she even saw them. It was a chilly, breezy, overcast day, not exactly as I'd envisioned. Mother Nature wasn't sticking to the plan!

When Leslie drove up, I scattered the rose petals around the deck and awaited her arrival. I rehearsed my speech one final time, in case the first nineteen weren't sufficient. When Leslie walked in the front door, her mom dutifully followed the plan and invited her upstairs to show her the work her dad had done on the third floor. I was listening at the top of the stairs and I heard Leslie ask, "What'd you want to talk to me about? Are you sick? Is Daddy sick?" Her mom assured her everyone was in the best of health.

I was fighting a losing battle with the rose petals. The wind was blowing them in every direction, as I pitifully tried to corral them all. I felt like I was on a game show in one of those booths filled with cash blown around by fans and I had to stuff as many bills as possible into my pants and shirt before the timer buzzed. I wasn't winning. Petals started flying off the deck, and as Leslie and her mom walked up the stairs, Leslie glanced out the window and asked, "Are those rose petals? Where'd they come from?" Her mom merely shrugged and kept walking.

When they reached the third floor, Leslie saw the deck door open and asked why it wasn't closed. But instead of leading her out onto the deck as planned, her mom shut the door. I stood there on the deck shivering in my suit with rose petals in my hands and pockets trying to figure out what had just happened. Was this her mom's way of telling me she really didn't want me in the family? Was it a signal to abort and regroup for a later time? Was I supposed to rappel down from the deck?

Suddenly, the door reopened and Zip, Leslie's parents' dog, trotted out. Was he the best they could offer? Or was I supposed to practice proposing to him? He came over and stood right next to me looking up, apparently eager to hear my finest pitch. Then Leslie's head appeared. She simply poked it out because her mom had told her to look at something on the deck. When she saw me, she turned to her mom and said, "What's he doing here?"

Nope, not exactly according to plan.

Then she tried to leave, but her mom grabbed her and began pushing her out onto the deck. What in the world was going on? The plan had been scrapped for a wrestling match.

Leslie later told me that when she saw me, she knew what was about to happen and she wished she'd dressed better (she was in scrubs, as usual) and put on more makeup. Thankfully, her mom stopped her and shoved her onto the deck because I couldn't have handled it any longer out there by myself.

Leslie cautiously approached like I might hurl her over the guardrail. I invited her to sit in the chair, while Zip lay beside her. I hoped he was comfortable. He certainly had a ringside seat. I got down on one knee just like in the movies, held Leslie's left hand, and delivered my speech.

But she didn't answer. Had I skipped a part? Was the question unclear? She just stared at me, crying. I didn't know what else to do, so I took it from the top again. This time, when I reached the part where she was supposed to chime in with an answer, she nodded, crying harder, and mumbled, "Okay."

When I slipped the ring on her finger, it was too loose. We later took it to be sized correctly, yet they botched the job and left us with no other option but to melt it down to make my ring out of hers. We then had to pick out another ring for Leslie. I told her, "Well, at least it'll make a good story one day. I'm wearing your ring."

My plan hadn't worked out precisely as prepared, but at least she was surprised, which was an accomplishment. She swore she had no clue I was there, which had been evident from her reaction. Maybe I should've warned her. She might've been a little more excited to see me.

We set a tentative date and began making plans. It all felt surreal. We were engaged and would soon be married. It seemed like a month ago we'd started writing each other letters. Didn't I just find her phone number on that box when she panicked and said goodbye? It was intimidating how fast time moved once something was set in motion. It made me feel tiny.

I'd decided to ask her because, despite my fears, uncertainties, and inability to map out the future down to the smallest details, I knew I'd never find anyone who wanted to be with me more than Leslie. It was impossible. For some odd reason, she loved me that much, and I would've regretted letting her go. Whatever struggles we encountered down the road couldn't equal the loss of that degree of adoration. When I looked at it that way, it was actually a pretty simple choice.

Leslie already knew where she wanted the wedding: right here at her folks' house out in the yard. They had lots of open land, which sounded good to me. Plus, we didn't need to buy flowers since the yard was already littered with roses.

He was a long way from losing it. Back in the salad days of our first band, Tripp and I used to drive for rehearsal to Texas Wesleyan

University where Bryan worked and lived as a dorm manager, and one evening, he greeted us with this warning: "I'm telling you right now, I'm fixin' to lose it." Tripp and I looked at each other like maybe we needed to cancel practice.

Yet now Bryan was graduating from seminary.

He'd survived practicum—actually, he'd flourished in it and gotten straight A's his last few semesters. His GPA had risen like it was riding an elevator. He'd earned his master of arts in marriage and family counseling, and since the graduation ceremony was during the week, I asked Richard if we could attend. Naturally, he said yes because he was so accommodating, yet he'd also become friends with Bryan, having chatted with him several times over the years.

Change was in the air, and Richard knew things were concluding and beginning all around him. He'd handled the news that I was getting married and would be leaving soon with a classic response: "What took you so long?"

I laughed and said, "I can't keep up with you. Nobody can."

Richard was far more concerned with how Bryan would fare once I left. He feared that the moment something went wrong and I wasn't around to support him, Bryan would slide into old patterns. But this time felt different than past years when we separated. Bryan was stronger now, more confident, healthier mentally and emotionally, and he had found his niche in counseling. He was good at it and enjoyed helping people. He felt like his struggles made him more empathetic and enlightened to clients' problems. He liked being needed and not the other way around. Now he was the one people turned to for help, which suited him just fine.

He even had a job lined up at a local counseling/neurofeedback center, which excited him because he believed the combination of both approaches was essential to a client's permanent progress. Neurofeedback directly trained brain function so it could actually learn to operate more efficiently. He said instead of merely walking a client through a crisis to a better place, they could fix the wiring to avoid repeating the same mistakes.

Bryan was in a good place and had come a long way, and his parents, who were seated near the front of the auditorium at his graduation, couldn't have been prouder. Richard and I chose to sit in the balcony because it offered more space for Richard to maneuver his wheelchair. Even seated far from the stage, it wasn't difficult to pick out Bryan when his graduating class stood because, at six-feet-four, he towered over most of them. I pointed him out to Richard, who simply looked up at me and said, "I've got CP, I'm not blind."

Since no one was sitting behind us, I stood for the ceremony, partly to see better and partly because I was so thrilled. I felt like a dad watching my son graduate. I kept thinking about Bryan sitting in his car years ago in a parking lot late at night contemplating suicide. It had happened more than once. I remembered his arrests, the ill-fated ATM caper. I thought about the first few semesters when he almost quit, about him sleeping in the work truck at the back of campus after being denied practicum, and about where he might've wound up if he'd left. I thought about his flashlight taped to his cap so he could study as we drove home from Dallas, the light under his door in the middle of the night because he had to finish a paper, his fist raised triumphantly when I told him he'd gotten into practicum.

I thought about him chasing me all over campus after we'd first met until I gave in and became his friend, the dreams we tossed around about where our band would one day go, the constant encouragement he'd given me to keep writing, the countless movie and pizza nights. I'd spent nearly twenty years with him, and without me even realizing, he'd become my closest friend and, even more, my support. I needed him just as much as he ever needed me, and I wondered where I might've wound up if it hadn't been for him.

I watched him step on stage with his mortarboard precariously perched on his head, and as tears welled in my eyes, I couldn't help but yell out, "Way to go, Bryan! You did it! *You did it!*" Richard looked at me, along with a few others nearby, yet in that moment I really didn't care how big of a scene I made. I couldn't help myself. They'd all just have to understand. I wasn't shouting congratulations, but gratitude. I was thanking the tall guy who just shook the commencement speaker's hand and waved awkwardly to his family. He was a friend of mine. The best kind. He'd stuck by me no matter how big of a jerk I was. He'd believed in me when I didn't. He'd carried me for a long time without acknowledgement, so the least I could do was scream thank you. He deserved much more, but it was all I had to offer. It was enough for him, though. He didn't want a big fuss. He was satisfied not to have tripped on stage. He was just happy to be there, with his friends and family, no longer where he'd once been. So was I. It had been a long road for both of us.

Our last lunch at Julie's was the hardest part of leaving, not just Richard but Fort Worth. Packing boxes, wrapping up loose ends, and making wedding plans (well, listening to Leslie's plans—she had a grand, master blueprint all mapped out for an outdoor, country wedding that required little from me other than agreement and following instructions) was the easy part, even fun because I was embarking on a new adventure. It was exciting to be getting married. I'd seen so many movies about weddings, it was finally my turn to experience it for myself.

The last few times Bryan, Todd, and I met to play tennis and pray were some of our most enjoyable Friday get-togethers. We knew this was our last chance to hang out as a group, at least consistently, so we made the most of it. Bryan's mom cooked all my favorite meals my last week in town, like she was concerned Memphis had a food shortage. Della deep-fried some French fries in peanut oil for old time's sake, and we squeezed in a final trip to the zoo to watch Richard and the lions have a staring contest. It was all a lot less painful than anticipated.

Until Julie's.

At first, it was a typical lunch. We talked with Amy as she pinballed from table to table, Jody stopped by to chat with Richard for a minute, I ate a tuna sandwich while Richard savored his chicken salad, roll, and sweet tea. We reminisced a bit. Amy asked about my wedding plans. I told her Federer wasn't invited, which she said was okay because Nadal wasn't welcome at Julie's.

Yet when it was time to leave, the weight of it all finally hit me, and Richard. Amy, too. It felt like our family was breaking up. All of the years spent reaching this level of comfortableness and camaraderie would vanish as soon as I pulled away in my U-Haul truck. I'd lived long enough to know these kinds of relationships didn't come along often. They were rare and needed to be appreciated, cultivated, and hung onto as long as possible. I understood wonderful people I loved awaited my arrival in Memphis. I wasn't being dropped off in an alley not knowing a soul. But that didn't make walking out of Julie's any less painful.

Amy stood holding the door open for Richard, who was already bawling. The knot in my throat felt like I'd swallowed a peach. Amy was fighting back tears, and when I said goodbye, I handed her a card I'd written telling her how much her friendship had meant to me and how grateful I was for her generosity toward Richard. She said she'd have to read it later because it was too much right now, for which I was thankful because I was barely holding it together. She and I hugged, and she whispered, "You're coming back, right? Before you leave?"

I nodded and said I would, then walked out with Richard. But I never did. In the hustle and bustle of last-minute errands and details, I ran out of time and didn't stop by Julie's once more to see Amy, and I regretted it for quite a while. I texted her to apologize and she, of course, assured me it was no big deal, yet I still felt guilty. Amy would've made time. Richard, too. Being around both of them had taught me that people should always come first, and often the most meaningful gesture was the sacrifice of a little time. Bryan had demonstrated this as well. Clearly, though, despite all their fine examples, I hadn't fully grasped this lesson.

My last afternoon with Richard was a quiet one. A few phone calls, a letter or two. A lot of silence. How could we tie a neat bow on five years? How did a cruise ship dock at a fishing pier? Finally, I asked him, "Have you picked out your suit yet? You better look sharp."

He smiled, and answered, "Don't I always?"

"Just let Della choose it."

"I'm gonna get a horn for my chair and blow it when we get there."

"Don't make us change the date."

He laughed and shrugged. "I'll show up every Saturday."

"That sounds like a horror movie."

He laughed even harder, and before he even started coughing, I stood up to get his cup.

We sat for a minute or so in silence again. It was almost time for me to leave. I'd been sitting next to him for so long, it was hard to believe there was a time when it felt awkward and uncomfortable. I'd thought I wouldn't last a month with him, and here we were years later trying to imagine the next day without each other. I was glad I hadn't listened to my fears. They were rarely valid.

I knew Richard would be okay. He'd survived many years without me. Plus, now he had Della, who brought him more joy than anyone else. But it was never easy to lose a buddy, and we both understood our years together had been a gift that wouldn't come around again. It was too unique of a relationship, too unexpected and unplanned. It was more than either of us could've hoped for when I showed up on his driveway, scared to enter his house. If someone had told us we'd both help each other find our wives, we would've had that unfortunate soul committed. If someone else had strolled passed and informed us we'd work together for five years, Richard would earn a master's degree, and I'd learn more about life than in all my years before (or since), that sad sack would've become roommates with the first one we committed.

But nothing great lasted forever because greatness was eventually replaced by nostalgia. There were lots of bands still out on the road that had once been on top of the charts but were now sentimental favorites. Richard and I had had a good run, but it was time to pack it in.

Though I easily could've worked for him for another five years, maybe ten. We had that much fun together.

Richard opened the front door for me using his automatic door opener and asked me to let him know when I arrived safely in Memphis. I assured him I would. I looked at my car that I was leaving Bryan (which felt a bit cruel since it would probably break down in another few months) and then turned back to Richard. I leaned down and gave him a hug and said, "Thanks for hiring me. You weren't half-bad to work for."

He smiled and replied, "I took it easy on you."

I nodded, fighting back tears, and said, "Glad you did. I needed the help."

He said, still smiling, "I know."

Then I nodded once more to thank him for more than I could find sufficient words for, and I walked down his driveway to my car. He followed me down and decided to drive in front of me as I slowly made my way out of his neighborhood, like a police escort clearing my passage. His orange light glowed as he sat up proudly leading our caravan. When I reached the corner of the main road, I pulled next to him and lowered my window and said, "Don't get hit out here."

"I'm too fast," he declared, zipping across the street toward CVS. I turned right and drove off, yet I could still see his orange light in my rearview mirror until he disappeared into the store. I watched for his light to reappear before he was out of view, but I drove down a hill and he was gone, undoubtedly inside presenting the manager with a proposition.

CHAPTER TWENTY

A Part-Time Job

Not long after I left, Richard and Della decided to move, too. They'd discussed it off and on ever since Evelyn and Emilee left for Tennessee, but they couldn't find a state in the general vicinity of Della's family that offered a reasonable assistance program for Richard.

I'd hoped they'd leave, even encouraged it. I helped Richard research other state programs, hunting for an acceptable landing spot that allowed Della to be near her family while addressing Richard's needs. At first, Richard wasn't too keen on the idea. Nothing we found offered what he currently received in Texas, and he'd invested so much time and energy on his program, while establishing a network of connections in the DFW Metroplex, it was too much to abandon.

Quietly, I'd urged him to reconsider. "Della will never leave you," I'd said with complete candor just a week before I left, "but if you want her to be happy, you need to bend a little here. You have to get her closer to home." He understood, even agreed, yet we hadn't found a suitable site.

Two days before I left, we were able to learn some valuable and promising information from one of the directors of the state program in North Carolina. Della's parents and siblings all lived in or near Kernersville, North Carolina, which was only six and a half hours from her kids in Manchester, Tennessee. One of her brothers lived in nearby Winston-Salem, which had sidewalks and a bus system, and there was an available house near his. Suddenly, Winston-Salem started looking like a viable option.

It didn't take them long to iron out the details and fast-track their move. Naturally, Della was thrilled, while Richard remained slightly less ebullient. However, this was understandable, as Della was heading back to family and Richard venturing into the imposing unknown. Plus, there was the whole Michael issue. He had no interest in leaving his friends, school, and home. He didn't know anyone in North Carolina. His brother and sister were in Texas. He'd spent his whole life in Fort Worth. It felt unfair to Richard to force him to go. He'd seen how homesickness plagued Evelyn and Emilee, and the sacrifice Della had made to let them leave. After much agonizing thought and prayer, Richard decided to let Michael move in with close family friends in Fort Worth who loved Michael and were ecstatic to have him. It was one of the hardest things Richard had ever done, and he was racked with guilt. But he understood that if he made Michael go with them, he would've felt guilty about that instead. Either choice left him regretful. At least this way, Michael was happy.

To his credit, Richard put on a brave face and said goodbye to Amy and Jody (poor Amy was losing everybody), John and his Healthcare Store crew, and his beloved Hulen Street shops to follow his wife to the east coast to rebuild his network. Fortunately for Richard, he'd never met a stranger, and the citizens of Winston-Salem had no idea who was about to hit town.

While Richard and Della were juggling relocating their lives, Leslie, I, and her family were busy preparing for our country wedding. It was no small undertaking. We'd lined up a fireworks display for after the reception; a massive tent to cover the tables and food; musicians to perform before, during, and after the ceremony; a delicious catered feast; an assortment of cakes from Muddy's Bake Shop; and about a hundred guests using GPS to find the remote house in the country.

Yet it was the little details that took much of our time and made the biggest difference. This is where Leslie's creativity really shone. She had her mother, an excellent artist, draw a picture of a tree, and then they framed it and set it out with ink pads for guests to leave their thumbprints (along with their signatures) on the branches of the tree. This was how they signed in, which I thought was clever. Her mom also wrote out the entire menu in calligraphy on a framed chalkboard.

The ceremony was in the front yard off to the side, so Leslie's dad built a gate through which everyone could enter. On top of the gate we spelled out in sticks the Bible verse John 1:16: "From the fullness of His grace, we have all received one blessing after another."

Under the tent, each table had milk glass and silver pitchers that Leslie had accumulated over time, along with vintage plates we'd rented. Croquet and horseshoes were set up on the lawn. All four of my groomsmen, Bryan, Todd, Tripp, and my old friend, Brian, who'd grown up with me at our church in D.C., wore matching blue-and-green striped socks and ties, while Leslie's four bridesmaids, Elisabeth, Emily, Dorothy, and her cousin, Opal, wore matching ankle-breaker tall wedges that Elisabeth had picked for them to teeter in across the uneven yard. Emily almost nosedived wobbling her way down the aisle.

My two significant contributions to the festivities were I picked the day and the yard. I researched the previous five years of weather for that month and chose the weekend that had consistently been the nicest. Also, Leslie had considered holding the wedding in the back yard, but I insisted the front yard offered more space and far less of her dad's scrap metal. In the end, the weather was perfect that weekend, and the front yard was a much cleaner choice. I was quite proud of myself but far more relieved. I'd been studying weather forecasts every few hours all week.

Jim, my old youth pastor who'd worked with Brian and me many years before, traveled to perform the ceremony. My parents came down from Cape Cod, as well as Gordon and Andy with their families. My other brother, David, wasn't able to attend, along with a few other old friends who couldn't untie themselves from previous commitments.

Unfortunately, this included Richard and Della.

They were literally right in the middle of their move that weekend and had to turn in their truck and supplies by Sunday. It was too far out of their way to make it in time. I understood, and when I talked to them on the phone, I assured them it was okay and they shouldn't feel an ounce of guilt. But I still missed them and wished they could've seen me get married, as I'd watched them. Della could've even sung "You Are So Beautiful" while we waited patiently at the altar, for a little payback.

Leslie cried as we exchanged vows, and I managed to make it through without stumbling my lines. She looked gorgeous, and the entire affair felt surreal, like I was sitting on the front porch watching it unfold. Yet it was really happening, and nobody objected to halt the proceedings before Jim made it official. We were married.

Five years earlier, marriage had been near the bottom of my to-do list. I wasn't ready. I had nothing to offer. What had changed in that time? Was I more successful? No. Were my prospects now limitless? Hardly.

But was I the same person who'd seen the notice in the break room for a tutor, and then met the man with cerebral palsy who would forever change my life? Not even close. My years with Richard had shifted my course and reshaped me, and as Leslie and I walked up the aisle holding hands and smiling at everyone, I wished my old boss were here to see it, without his horn. He would've probably tried to escort us out until Della locked his wheels. It would've made for a great photo.

As I looked around at my parents and family—and my new family—and all the friends gathered, I felt grateful to have made it here, past my best line of defense, all the way to the bottom where the longest safety line couldn't stretch and I could finally see. I felt home, at last. And I couldn't help but chuckle that all of this had started with a part-time job I didn't even want, yet needed more than I ever could've imagined.

Leslie and I, now happily married parents of two.

Above: With Bryan at my wedding.
Right: Michael, Richard, and Della enjoying a dip in the pool.